HOW TO BUILD A SUCCESSFUL LIFE IN SPITE OF YOURSELF

Publisher's Name: John Turben

ISBN: 978-1-962142-44-1

Contents

PART ONE
BUILDING A
SUCCESSFUL LIFE:
THE EARLY YEARS

CHAPTER ONE
WHEN LIFE KNOCKS YOU DOWN, GET BACK UP

Into every life, some rain must fall.

We've all heard that old proverb. And most of us have seen enough to know that it's true.

Everyone has his or her share of disappointment and success. We have been through bright, sunny days full of joy. And we have all been stuck in dark valleys where it seemed that it would never stop raining.

But why do some people let their failures push them down to the point where they become victims – anxious and afraid, seemingly always waiting for the next blow to land.

And why is it that other people let their disappointments roll off their shoulders. When life knocks them down, they get back on their feet immediately, like a prizefighter who refuses to go down for the count.

Why are some people crushed by the unkindness and cruelty they encounter, while others are able to say, "I don't care what others may think of me, or say about me. I know I'm going to succeed"?

My purpose in writing this book is, as the title says, to show you how you can build a successful, fulfilling life. What I'm going to tell you is borne out in my personal experience, and in years spent as a hypnotherapist, during which I helped thousands of my clients overcome anxiety and fear.

I am writing both for adults who want to succeed in life, and for parents who want to help their children fulfill their in-born potential and become everything they are capable of being.

IT'S NEVER TOO LATE

The process of building a successful life begins in early childhood – and even before birth. Children who are still in the womb can be affected by their environment and the mental state of their mothers. They may be traumatized by a loud, angry, or unhappy situation, and they may be comforted by a calm, happy peaceful one.

But the good news is that what happens to us in those early years doesn't have to determine the path we'll follow for the rest of our lives. No matter how old you are, it's never too late to get on the right track.

My own life is a case in point. As a child, I never seemed to fit in. I was picked on and bullied mercilessly by other children in my neighborhood. Why? Was it because there was something wrong with me? Not really. It's just that my self-confidence was very low. If the other kids said something terrible about me, I felt it must be true and so did not do a good job of standing up for myself – and the person who won't stand up for himself or herself is perceived as an easy mark. By the time I grew up, I had post-traumatic stress disorder and was addicted to crack cocaine, which I had used to numb my feelings, so I didn't have to deal with my hurt and pain. I had also been diagnosed with bipolar disorder.

It was only when I discovered my worth as a human being that my life began to change.

I went on to a successful career as an entertainer, appearing as a hypnotist in clubs throughout the Midwestern United States. Ultimately, I decided that I wanted to use my skills as a hypnotist, to do more than entertain people, so I opened my private practice as a hypnotherapist.

It wasn't that simple, of course. There were years of training and education before I was able to "hang out my shingle" and start helping people heal from the trauma they had experienced in their childhoods.

AS THE TWIG IS BENT. . .

In order to explain how to build a successful life, we must start at the beginning – in other words, with the first five years. It is often said, "As the twig is bent, so grows the tree." And it is true that what happens to us in the first few years shapes who we are as adults. Aristotle famously said, "Give me a child until he is seven, and I will show you the man." As you would expect, Aristotle generally got it right, although, as I said, it is possible to undo what has been done in the early years and get on the path to success.

Over the past few years, several scientific studies have found that the first three years of a child's life are especially important with regard to future academic and social success. It is during this time that children begin to have playdates and learn how to get along with other children. This is when they start to learn about letters and numbers and put words together in sentences. By the time a child is three years old, the brain has grown to 80 percent of its final size. By the age of five, the brain is 90 percent of the size it will be during adulthood. Renowned psychologist Bonny Forrest writes, "In these early years, what matters most is a foundation of supportive relationships that allows a child to feel secure and confident as she explores her world. These relationships with sensitive caregivers are the most important factor in determining a child's ability to be successful later in life. In my own practice, I constantly see the long-standing impact that our earliest relationships have on us."[1]

Still, as a general rule, parents must understand that children are fragile creatures and treat them as such. It is not true that little boys and girls have short memories, and so will forget traumatic things that have been said or done to them. By the time a person reaches their teen years, he most likely will not seem to remember anything that happened to him before the age of three. But those events that happened in the first couple of years of life — or at least the effects of those events —are still there in the subconscious, shaping the thoughts and behaviors of the adult. A harsh putdown from his mother or father when the child was two years old may stay in a child's subconscious until he is in his 50s or 60s. Perhaps even longer. I have known people who spent their entire lives trying to please a harsh and demanding parent, even long after that parent had died.

I recall a man – I'll call him Joe – who struggled with feelings of inferiority. He thought he was inept and helpless, and so he was. Why did he think of himself this way? Because this was what he had been told from the earliest days of his life — or at least this was what he thought he had been told.

I hypnotized him and told him to see himself as a baby, surrounded by everyone in his family. I asked him to listen to them telling him how much they loved him, how proud they were of him, and how they expected great things from him. We did this several times over a period of many weeks, and as the scene became implanted in his mind, his self-confidence began to grow and his behavior changed.

Self-confidence has so much to do with success in life. The person who thinks he or she is going to fail is likely to do just that. Children need to be loved and encouraged. They need to be embraced and told they are worthy of respect and honor. You can do your young child a huge favor by letting her know that she will be capable of handling all the circumstances that life will bring her way. I'm not saying that self-respect makes all the difference between success and failure, but it does have a lot to do with it.

Self-confidence is not to be confused with arrogance, bravado or being loud and aggressive. Self-confidence is a quiet, steady belief in yourself. It is coming to a difficult situation and thinking, "I can handle this," rather than throwing your hands up in a panic and saying, "I give up. I'm doomed."

Self-confidence is believing in yourself enough to put in the hard work it takes to accomplish whatever it is that needs to be done. And that kind of attitude starts in early childhood. There is plenty of proof that having a positive attitude about yourself can make a huge difference in your performance. For example, in his book, *Emotional Intelligence*, Daniel Goleman tells of a study of swimmers that was conducted at the University of Pennsylvania.2 The study involved several members of the university's swim team. Previous studies had revealed which of the swimmers tended to be confident and optimistic, and which were pessimistic.

After judges timed the swimmers' performances in a special competition, all of the athletes were told that they had performed worse than they actually did. They were also asked to rest up for a while, and then give it another try. The swimmers who believed in themselves improved their performances during the second attempt, even though they had really done very well the first time. Those who were pessimistic uniformly did worse during their second attempt. We see from this and many similar studies that self-confidence is an important ingredient in personal success. And, again, self-confidence is, to a great extent, an outcome of a healthy childhood.

As Goleman says, "Optimism, like hope, means having a strong expectation, that, in general, things will turn out all right in life, despite setbacks and frustrations. From the standpoint of emotional intelligence, optimism is an attitude that buffers people against falling into apathy, hopelessness, or depression in the face of tough going. And, as with hope, its near cousin, optimism pays dividends in life (providing, of course, it is a realistic optimism; a too-naïve optimism can be disastrous."3

That last point is important. Don't tell your child that she is good at endeavors for which she has no real aptitude. Look for areas where aptitude really does exist and encourage your child in those.

Perhaps you saw the movie that came out a few years ago, *Florence Foster Jenkins*, in which Meryl Streep played a woman who thought she had a beautiful singing voice, but was actually one of those people who can't carry a tune in a bucket. Her encouraging husband even rented large auditoriums where she could perform. People were laughing behind her back, but she never knew it. Of course, the movie was a light-hearted comedy. But it is sad to see someone who has channeled all their energy into an area where they have little or no ability.

So don't lie to your children about how great they are in a particular area. Most of the time, they will see right through flattery. But, of course, always look for ways to compliment their intelligence, creativity and ability to get things done. Here are some words you should never say to your child:

"Stupid."

"Lazy."

"Helpless."

"Bad."

"Idiot."

"Disappointment."

I'm sure you can think of many more.

I urge you to stop and count to ten – or twenty – whenever you feel tempted to use any of these words to describe your child or his or her behavior.

Children can be and are affected by negativity on the part of their parents. There is a misperception that childhood is a happy, carefree time of life, but this is not true for many boys and girls. In fact, in a 2009 study of 306 preschool children from ages three to six, 75 of them were found to be severely depressed. Other studies have found that children born to mothers who are depressed are often depressed themselves. For example, one study of surviving women who were pregnant and working at the World Trade Center during the 9/11 terrorist attacks, found that the children who were born to them had a lower-than-average amount of a hormone called cortisol, which helps to control stress and anxiety. Even though the children had not been born when the attack occurred, they were affected by it and had anxiety because of it.

So, what do we do to prevent our children from stress and anxiety? Do we go around walking on eggshells, being careful not to say or think anything the least bit negative? Well, that may not be a bad idea, but it's not very practical in this broken world of ours. Nor is it practical to hover over our children at all times, seeking to protect them from harm. Stubbed toes and broken hearts are a natural part of life, and our goal must be to learn how to deal with them, rather than avoid them altogether.

But parents must remember that their actions have consequences. It's okay to make mistakes, but even the smallest children deserve an apology when they have been wronged in some way.

We also must remember that children are children and not expect them to act like little adults. They are easily frightened and should be comforted and talked to as gently and honestly as possible. They should not be berated and told to quit acting like babies. If they act like babies, it's because they *are* babies. In his book, *The Worried Child*, Dr. Paul Foxman writes that, "any childhood experience involving a fear reaction or threat to security can develop into an anxiety disorder. Such experiences can include the following:

- Seeing a gun or other weapon
- Seeing violence on television or in movies
- Divorce of parents
- Violence in the home (often caused by alcoholism)
- Becoming sick and vomiting
- A serious or painful injury
- Illness in a parent
- Sexual or physical abuse
- Natural disasters."

Any of these things can cause emotional wounds that must be treated with care and understanding. Instead, some children are told, "It's no big deal. Get over it!" But it is a big deal, and can fester and become an even bigger deal if not dealt with properly.

DEALING WITH YOUR OWN CHILDHOOD TRAUMA

What if your parents didn't know how to deal with childhood trauma, and left you to deal with your wounds on your own? Or, even worse, what if they were the source of your emotional injuries? What can you do if you left the years of teddy bears and tea parties behind a long, long time ago, but you're still feeling the pain of what happened to you then? In that case, I am convinced that a good therapist, and especially a good hypnotherapist, could help you find healing and hope. But there are some steps you can take to help yourself.

The first thing I suggest is for you to find a peaceful spot where you can be completely alone with your thoughts. Then center your thoughts around a particular incident that has troubled you for years. (If there are many such incidents – and there probably are – then you may have to repeat this process numerous times.) The next step is to think back on what happened, reviewing the incident with as much detail as possible. In fact, if you can, please do what I would have you do if I had put you under hypnosis. Try, in your mind, to go back to the moment of the trauma, and relive it as if you are actually there now.

At you do this, a number of emotions will undoubtedly rise up in you. Take some time to think about what you're feeling and why. Don't try to stifle what you're feeling or run from it. Let it flow. Experience it.

Also, think about what you might have done to change the situation. Were you afraid to speak up and defend yourself? Then, picture yourself doing that now. Did you run away from someone who was bullying you? Then imagine yourself staying and fighting. In other words, do your best to remake the memory into what you wish had happened.

As you think deeply about this point of crisis, consider how it has affected you. For example, how has it changed the way you view yourself? How has it impacted the way you view others? Has it made you angry, sad, or caused you to be withdrawn or overly aggressive? If so, what steps can you take to overcome in the areas where you struggle? Is there someone you need to confront, or apologize to? (I don't recommend confronting, unless it is necessary or can be done in a gentle, constructive way. We are seeking healing, and not any sort of revenge or retribution.) If you are unable to confront the person who hurt you – for instance if your father hurt you by the things he said to you, but is no longer living, select a trustworthy friend and ask him or her to play the role of your father. He or she can help you by listening as you pour out your feelings and even apologize on behalf of the person who wronged you.

You may also find relief in writing letters to those who have wronged you. You don't have to send them and, in most instances, probably shouldn't. Again, our goal is for you to heal, and not inflict pain on others.

I understand that this may sound a bit simplistic to some people, but it works. It can have the same effect as lancing a boil that has been festering in your psyche for years.

Another action I would suggest is journaling, writing things down on paper. Often, as we write, emotions and feelings come to the forefront that we didn't know were there. As you write, you may recall events that change your perspective on past events.

The final step is to let go of your wounded emotions. Some people need a ritual to help them do this. If you feel this would help, you may write down a description of the event you are releasing, burn the paper, and then scatter the ashes. You might also write a letter, to the person who wronged you, burn it and scatter or bury the ashes. I have also heard of people scattering seed in a river or stream and watching as the current carries it away. It doesn't really matter what you do. The idea is to take some sort of symbolic action in order to obtain closure on the pains that have bothered you so long.

FOOD FOR THOUGHT

- It is often true that what happens to us in the first few years of life shapes who we are as adults. What are some of the experiences that have shaped who you are?
- A child's early experiences are especially important to his or her future academic and social success. Why do you think this is so?
- Having a positive attitude about yourself as a child can make a great difference in your performance as an adult. What can you do to help your child develop a positive attitude?

Remember:

- Self-confidence is one of the most important outcomes of a healthy childhood.
- Any childhood experience that involves a fear reaction or a threat to security can develop into an anxiety disorder.

---

1 Forrest, Bonny, 'Will My Kid Grow Out of It?" (Chicago: Chicago Review Press) 2014, Page 121 2 Goleman, Daniel, "Emotional Intelligence," (New York: Bantam Books) 1995, Page 88 3 Goleman, Page 88.

CHAPTER TWO
THE TROUBLED CHILD

If you were offered the chance to go back and relive your childhood, would you do it?

Most people say no. They don't even have to think about it very long.

For most of us, childhood had way too many troubles. Some of us struggled to keep up in school. Others were tormented by bullies. We worried that we would never be able to meet our parents' expectations. Or that other kids wouldn't like us. And some had far worse situations to deal with – like verbal and physical abuse at the hands of their parents.

No, childhood is not exactly the way it's portrayed in a Walt Disney movie. Even those who look back upon it as a happy time start to change their view when they really stop and think about it.

The myth that childhood is full of fun and pleasure fades away when we realize that 8 percent of all children suffer from anxiety, which usually shows up about the age of six. Girls are more likely than boys to develop such a disorder.

Now, anxiety is not always such a bad thing. It is the body's alarm system that warns us when we're in danger, or that stirs us to be alert when we have something important to do —like taking a test or going to the dentist. But when anxiety is out of control, it can be a monster.

As you might expect, it is often the child who wants to please who falls victim to anxiety. These are usually boys and girls who have a strong sense of responsibility, who want their parents to be proud of them, who are oversensitive to criticism because it makes them feel that they are failing, and who have difficulty standing up for themselves.

I recently talked to a woman who told me what happened when her nine-year-old daughter came home from school with a grade of 97 out of 100 on a story she wrote for English class.

She was obviously upset, so her mom told her, "Honey, 97 is a very good score." "No, it's not," said her daughter, sobbing. "Now I'll never be able to get into a decent college, and I'll probably wind up living on the street."

That sort of overreaction is typical of children with anxiety disorder. Setbacks are magnified many times over. Achievements are never enough. And unless the child gets the therapy she needs, she is likely to struggle with anxiety in some way or another for the rest of her life.

Here are five things you can do to help a child who is struggling with anxiety:

1) Help them face their fears

First, you can help him face his fears head-on, instead of trying to run away from them. Trying to avoid stressful situations only makes them seem bigger and scarier. Instead, if a child faces his fears, he will learn that the anxiety reduces naturally over time. Usually, it will begin to subside within 20 to 45 minutes. It's a bit like tasting a vegetable for the first time. You can't know you don't like it if you won't even try it.

2) Give them a break

Second, you can take it easy on them by letting them know you don't expect them to be perfect in every situation. Over the last few years, there has been a lot of talk about "Tiger Moms" who are relentless in pushing their children toward success. Much has been written about how successful the children of these parents are. And while it may be true that they seem to perform well in academics, music, and other areas where they are pushed to excel, I doubt very much if any of them will become well-adjusted, happy adults. I have seen enough to believe that continual stress and pressure will invariably lead to an emotional breakdown. What are you gaining or accomplishing if your child gets straight A's all the way through school, becomes valedictorian of his or her high school, goes off to an Ivy

League college, and then has to undergo years of therapy to deal with the trauma caused by all that pressure? Is it worth the cost? I don't think so.

I am not saying you shouldn't teach your children to do their best. Don't allow your son or daughter to coast through school when he or she has the capability to excel. There is a thin line between expecting too much from your children and not expecting enough. That line is not always easy to find, but it is more than worth the effort you put into finding it.

3) Don't focus on the negatives

What do you do if your child brings home a report card with an A-plus in math and a C minus in science? Most of us focus on the lower grade. We pass right over the A and start asking why this science grade is so disappointing. Yes, of course, that C-minus needs to be improved, and it's important to talk about that. But not before you affirm your child for his stellar performance in math class.

Most people don't write letters or make phone calls to thank people for excellent service. But if we feel like we've been cheated or let down in some way, we're quick to complain. Just look at the letters to the editor in your local newspaper and see how many of them were written in anger. Negativity motivates us.

But our kids need us to look at the positive side of things.

Every good supervisor knows that if he needs to give a bit of bad news or criticism to an employee, the best way to deliver it is between two slices of good news or praise. You don't want to leave your employee thinking that he can't do anything right, making him so deflated he feels like giving up. In the same way, your kids need to hear the good news, too. As Bonny Forrest says, "Anxious and stressed children can get lost in negative thoughts and self-criticism. They may focus on how the glass is half empty instead of half-full and worry about future events. The more that you are able to focus on your child's positive attributes and the good aspects of a situation, the more that it will remind your child to focus on the positives."[4]

4)Let your child talk about it

It can be exasperating to deal with a child who suffers from anxiety. His or her irrational fears can wear you down, especially when it seems that you are going over the same old conversation again and again. But please remember that one of your jobs as a parent is to listen. It is not helpful to tell an anxious child that he is "being silly," or to "snap out of it." Listening sympathetically is one of the best things you can do. It's good to ask questions like, "I can see that this really bothers you. Can you tell me why?" And then work with him or her to find a solution to the problem. As Amy Przeworski writes in Psychology Today,

"This does not mean solving the problem for your child. It means helping your child to identify possible solutions. If your child can generate solutions, that is great. If not, generate some potential solutions for your child and ask him or her to pick the solution that he or she thinks would work best."

Over the last couple of years, the world seems to have rediscovered the wisdom of a man known as Mr. Rogers. There have been two best-selling books, and a movie based on the life of Fred Rogers. A soft-spoken, gentle man, Rogers became one of the best-known TV personalities of the 1970s and 80s. He loved children and wanted to help them overcome their fears and grow into healthy adults.

On his television show, Rogers often sang songs to help children overcome their fears and deal with difficult situations. One of these songs dealt with the fear of being sucked down the drain in the bathtub: "Oh you can't go down the drain. No, you can't go down the drain."

I admit, it sounds kind of silly. Surely, no child actually thinks he could go down the drain. Well, actually, yes, they do. And my point is that even though some children's fears may sound ridiculous to the adult mind, we mustn't laugh at them or ridicule them. Our job is to listen to them, discuss them seriously, and explain as clearly as we can why they cannot come true.

When you talk to your young child seriously about his fears, you are teaching him that he can always talk to you about anything – and that will be important in the years ahead.

5) Lead by Example

Turner is a happy, 18-month-old boy who seems to love everyone. Like all little boys, he gets his share of bumps and bruises. He gets knocked down from time to time by the family dog. He's also a bit of a daredevil, which adds to his collection of scrapes and cuts.

Usually, after he takes one of his falls and finds himself face-down on the hardwood floor, he looks around to see how his mom and dad are reacting. If they seem scared and upset, then he's scared and upset, too, crying and reaching out to be held. But if Mommy laughs and says, "Whee! Was that fun?" then he laughs along with her. Obviously, she wouldn't laugh if she thought her baby was hurt, but my point is that he takes his cues from her.

Our children are always watching us and learning how to react from how we react. If they see us get panicked over small issues, they will likely do the same thing. If they see us handle tough issues with poise and confidence, they will most likely learn how to do the same thing. I say "most likely" because there are no guarantees. There are exceptions to every rule, but in the vast majority of situations children will naturally follow their parents' behavior.

The bottom line is that when you want to reduce your child's anxiety, you must manage your own anxiety.

As you have been reading the five points above, I trust you have seen how every one of them can also apply to people who are no longer children. If you have been dealing with anxiety problems, or other issues stemming from childhood trauma, you can also benefit from fine-tuning these steps just a little bit and applying them to yourself.

1) Face your fears

One of the best things you can do when you start feeling anxious is to face your fears and float through them. Understand that panic will not consume you or kill you. You may feel bad right now, but it will pass. Your heartbeat will calm down. The butterflies will quit fluttering around in your stomach. Hang on, float through, and your anxiety will go away.

2) Give yourself a break

Superman is not a real person. Neither is Wonder Woman.

They are both fictional characters, so don't expect yourself to be like them. Real human beings make mistakes. They sometimes feel afraid. They have regrets. You are doing yourself a disservice if you expect to be perfect in every situation.

I have talked to many people who are far kinder to complete strangers than they are to themselves. They can overlook other people's faults but can't seem to overlook their own. I urge you to be kind to yourself. If you struggle in this area, it may help you to make a list of the things you are good at, or things you like about yourself. Then put it somewhere you can read it each morning or night. If this embarrasses you or strikes you as too egotistical, ask your spouse or a trusted friend to prepare the list. Reminding yourself of your strong points can go a long way toward helping you forgive yourself for your weaknesses.

3) Don't focus on the negatives

How do you talk to yourself? Do you get mad at yourself for being "inept" or "clumsy"? Do you call yourself "stupid" or "dumb"? If you do any of these things, please stop it now! I guarantee you that you are none of these things, and you must stop listening to the negative voices in your mind.

4) Talk about it

We previously discussed the importance of helping your children talk about their anxieties and fears. It is also crucial that adults with such issues talk about them, either with a professional therapist, a clergyman, or trusted friend. Perhaps I should say, "a very well trusted friend." The last thing anyone needs is to have their private issues spread around town by someone who doesn't know how to keep a secret. But, again, it is an important part of the healing process to share what you're going through with others.

Some people don't want to talk about their issues because they think that no one will understand. They feel, "Nobody has the issues I have. Nobody else has the weird thoughts that come into my head. People will think I'm crazy."

But it's not true. You are not alone. Your experiences are not unique. They are common to humankind, and you have no reason to be embarrassed or ashamed. As we share our innermost feelings, we develop a community that helps us move toward healing together. This is a huge benefit of group therapy, and of 12-Step programs like Alcoholics Anonymous and Celebrate Recovery, that have such a good record of helping people get free from drugs and alcohol. There is strength in numbers.

5) Find a good example

When we talked about helping our children, we discussed how important it is for parents to be good role models. Actually, having a good example to follow is important for everyone, and especially for those who grew up with parents who didn't know how to be positive role models.

And, believe me when I tell you, I've heard some wild stories. One young man in his 30s, told me that his father was a professional car thief who ran a chop shop out of their garage. Sometimes, after he and his sister were in their pajamas, they would get in their car and drive around town with their parents looking for cars to steal. When I asked him how old

he and his sister were at the time, he said, "Maybe six or seven." As I said, not all parents are good role models.

This is why I find such value in the role of sponsors, as used by such organizations as Alcoholics' Anonymous. It can be so helpful to know someone who has walked the road before you, someone who has succeeded and is able to say, with true conviction, "You can do it, too!" For example, if someone has been clean and sober for less than a week, imagine how good it feels to get connected to someone who has been fighting, and winning, the battle against addiction for over 10 years – to have someone you can call when you're tempted, and know that he or she will talk you through it. What a blessing!

At this point, you may be thinking, "Why are we talking so much about addiction? That's not my problem." I understand. But the principle applies to any issue you might be facing: anxiety, fear, low self-respect, depression … it means so much to have a mentor who understands what you are going through and can offer you the benefit of his or her own experience.

Where can you find a mentor? At your church. At school. At your workplace. In your neighborhood. Just about anywhere. But that doesn't mean it will be easy. You must take the time and care to make the right choice. And if you find that the person you choose isn't the right one after all, then start over!

FOOD FOR THOUGHT

- Eight percent of all children over the age of six suffer from an anxiety disorder. What can you do as a parent, to protect your children from anxiety?
- Parents must avoid focusing on the negative. Children need positive feedback. Can you think of some ways to give positive feedback, even when correction is called for?
- Children learn more from their parents' example than they learn from what their parents say. Can you think of some times when your parents' words and actions did not line up? Do you see some ways you should change your actions to better align with what you say to your children?
- If you face your fears head on, they will diminish over time. What does this mean to you personally?

Remember:

- It is often the child who wants to please who falls victim to anxiety.

PART TWO
SURVIVING THE
TEEN YEARS

4 Przeworski, Amy, Ph.D, "12 Steps to Reduce Your Child's Stress and Anxiety," Psychology Today, February 19, 2013

CHAPTER THREE

EXPLODING HORMONES AND MORE

Many people look back on their teenage years with a great deal of fondness. They remember those years as being filled with fun and adventure.

My response to that is, "Thank God for selective memories."

True, there are many good things to be said about the years "twixt twelve and twenty," but there are a lot of difficult things about that time of life as well. Like hormones, acne, social awkwardness, physical awkwardness, the constant effort of trying to fit in, dealing with changes in your body, learning how to get along with members of the opposite sex, and being stuck somewhere in the never-never land between childhood and adulthood.

I could probably go on for pages. . .but I won't. The teen years can also be difficult because life gets harder. School is more intense than it's ever been before, and in these days especially, teenagers are pushed harder than ever to succeed. It's almost reached the point where you can't get into a top college without a 4.0 GPA, a resume showing hundreds of hours of community service, and several outstanding accomplishments in arts, sports, or other related fields. I'm exaggerating, but not by much.

And then there are the bullies. Unfortunately, bullies are always a part of life, although the way they demonstrate their cruelty changes over the years. But sadly, there seem to be more of them during the teenage years, adding more difficulty to an already difficult time. The question is, how do we deal with issues like hormones, stress and bullies? How do we protect our children from their damage? And, If we ourselves are still carrying around trauma from our own experience as teenagers, how do we find healing and wholeness?

FINDING A GOOD THERAPIST

It's important for me to mention that even though you can do a great deal on your own, the solution to the problems we are discussing often involves finding and utilizing the work of a good therapist. A good therapist can find underlying causes that you may not be aware of. He or she can guide you through healing exercises, monitor your progress, and make clinical diagnoses.

But how do you find a therapist – one who has a proven track record and is just right for you? Here are a few suggestions:

1) Ask your friends and family

Do you have any friends or family members who are in therapy? If so, ask them how they feel about their therapists? And if you don't know anyone who is in therapy, ask your friends if they do. A personal referral can help a great deal. You can find out exactly what your friends like or don't like about their counselors, and it might even be that some of the things they don't like are things you would appreciate. As I've already mentioned, it's important to find a counselor that you are comfortable working with.

Do an online search

You may be able to find a good therapist in your area by checking out sites like *Psychology Today's Therapy Directory*. If you choose this route, be sure to read the reviews to find out what people like you feel about the therapist in question. By the way, whenever I'm looking at reviews, I try to read between the lines and not take everything that's said at face value. Some people have an axe to grind. Others would never think of saying a negative word about anyone. Still, if a therapist has dozens of top-flight reviews, you can be pretty sure that he – or she – knows what he's doing.

2) Have a conversation

Will your potential therapist allow you to come in for a free consultation? Or, if that's not possible for some reason, can you at least get on the phone for 15 minutes and talk about what you're looking for in a therapist? If not,

I suggest you continue your search elsewhere. What do you want to find out? Well, for starters, you need to know what they charge and if they will accept your insurance. Have they worked with people who have your particular issue? You might also ask where they got their degree and if he has a special area of expertise. After a brief conversation, you should be able to tell whether this is a person you would be comfortable with.

Here is some good advice from Seth Gillihan, Ph.D., writing in Psychology Today: 5

"While it can be daunting to find an excellent therapist, it may be one of the most important decisions you make when you or a family member is going through a difficult time. So, it's worth choosing carefully. . .

"On the other hand, there is no such thing as a perfect therapist — which I can certainly affirm from my own experience as a therapist — and every close relationship will have strengths and limitations. The aim isn't to find the *one* right therapist, but one who's a good fit and will provide skilled and compassionate support through a period of difficulty and growth."

Keep in mind that you have the right to switch to another therapist at any time. If the counselor you've chosen won't answer your questions or if you feel that they are condescending or dismissive in any way, then by all means tell them that you want to discontinue sessions with him.

It's crucial that you trust your therapist and feel comfortable with them. But please don't make major decisions hastily. Be patient. Don't expect everything to be worked out within a session or two.

THE MONSTER OF DEPRESSION

Now, let's take a quick look at some of the major issues connected with the teenage years, and talk about what you can do to overcome them. First of all, depression – and suicide. As you may know, suicide is among the top causes of death for American teenagers –- rating first in some reports and second in others. In fact, over the past few years, the number of teenage suicides in the United States has spiked, reaching the highest level since 1960. This has happened while deaths from other causes have dropped by one-third. Suicides have even been recorded among children as young as five or six years old, so the problem is obviously an epidemic. According to the Center for Disease Control, the suicide rate among American teenagers increased 76 percent in the decade between 2007 and 2017, a sobering and heartbreaking statistic.

Suicide has been called a permanent solution to a temporary problem. It is a drastic, heart-breaking step for a young person who may be feeling rejected, worthless and picked on.

It is not easy for parents to talk to their children about such a touchy subject as suicide, but it is vital. So how do parents know if their children are clinically depressed and thinking suicidal thoughts? Here are some behaviors to watch for:

1) Isolation

Has your child suddenly stopped hanging out with his or her friends?

Ruminating

Does he or she seem to be lost in thought all the time?

2) Loss of appetite

Does your teenager pick at his food? Is he suddenly turning up his nose at foods he has always loved? This can be a sign of serious trouble.

3) Sleeping too much or too little

It's not uncommon for teenagers to like to lie in bed in the morning. But if your teen has never done this before, and suddenly starts doing it, then something serious may be going on. Watch for changes in sleeping patterns. If you see some sudden, noticeable changes, ask him or her about it.

4) Poor performance in school

If your child's grades suddenly take a nosedive, that, too can be a sign of severe depression, – although there can be other things going on as well. It could be that your son or daughter has begun hanging out with friends who are not interested in academic success, or it could be that your child has begun drinking or using recreational drugs.

The bottom line is that if your child has always been a good student, and suddenly begins coming home with D's and F's, then something is happening, and you need to get to the bottom of it. Don't tell yourself, "Oh, she's just going through a phase. She'll get over it." Talk to your child and ask what's going on. Make appointments with teachers to get their point of view. And if the problem persists, seek out professional help.

5) Giving away possessions

Teenagers who are depressed and contemplating ending it all may start giving away their prized possessions. A favorite jacket or sweater. Video games or books. Other items with great sentimental value. Of course, most parents want their children to be generous and to think about the needs of others. But when a young person begins giving his belongings away, it may mean that he's thinking, "I'm not going to need these things anymore."

It is so important for parents to be alert and stay on top of the situation. We can't afford to bury our heads in the sand and tell ourselves, "My child would never. . . do this or that." Depression makes people do things they would otherwise never dream of doing.

I don't want to be alarmist. The last thing I want to do is scare anyone. What I do want is for you to be fully informed and prepared to deal with any serious issues that may arise.

Your child may be offended that you "worry so much" about him, or that you're "always on his back." So what? It's better for him to be offended than seriously injured – or dead.

I know of several occasions where parents have backed off because their child said, "How could you even think that I would harm myself? I would never do anything like that." Perhaps they meant it when they said it – but it didn't turn out to be true.

Again, don't worry about making your children angry with you. After all, you're the parent. That's what you're here for!

FOOD FOR THOUGHT

- **What if you need a therapist?** How do you find a good one?

Ask your friends and family for recommendations

Do an online search

Ask your prospective therapist for a consultation.

Remember:

- **If you decide you are not satisfied** with the therapist you have chosen, you have a right to switch to a new one.
- **Suicide is a top cause of teenage deaths in America.** Here are some danger signs to look out for:

Isolation

Rumination

Loss of appetite

Changes in sleep habits

Giving things away

₅ Seth Gillihan, "How Do You Find a Good Therapist?" Psychology Today.com/ November 7, 2018

CHAPTER FOUR

DEALING WITH BULLIES

Bullying has always been a serious issue, but it now seems to be worse than ever before. So much for the idea that human beings are evolving and becoming more caring of others. Unfortunately, there is no empirical evidence to support such a contention. Bullying is so serious that it deserves its own chapter.

Bullying and being bullied aren't necessarily a teenage phenomenon. Bullying occurs at all ages, but it does seem much worse during the adolescent and teenage years. And with the proliferation of digital media, bullying is easier than it's ever been before. Consider all the trolls who hide behind anonymity while they unleash their hatred on the internet. Sometimes it seems that our nation is full of cyber bullies who love nothing more than inflicting pain on others. What a tragic state of affairs!

SHARING MY OWN EXPERIENCE

Bullying is one of the reasons why I became a therapist. I was bullied incessantly when I was younger, and I wanted to help people who had suffered as I did. My interest in helping victims of bullying is much more than theoretical. It's personal. And I'm sharing my story with you because I want to let you know that, if you are being bullied in some way, you are not alone – and you can overcome!

For me, it started when I was a boy of nine or ten. There were some older boys who were really into cars and liked to hang out at a neighborhood service station. It seemed to me that they liked picking on children almost as much as they liked working on cars. For some reason, some of us thought they were cool and wanted to be like them. Looking back on it now, I can't imagine why. They would do things like pin my arms behind my back and twist them until I thought they were going to break, knock me down, call me names, and do whatever else they could think of that would inflict physical and emotional pain.

Truth be told, I was an easy mark. I was a scrawny little kid who struggled to stand up for myself. And, as is often true of bullies, when they saw how easy it was to pick on me, the "games" intensified. The rest of my school years were rough. I was picked on incessantly, and I had no one to defend me. My father was an alcoholic who was mean when he drank, which was just about all the time. My mother tried to help me, but she didn't really know how.

My high school years were so tough that I decided to quit a few months before graduation and join the Air Force. My mother was not happy with my decision, to say the least, but I was 18, so there wasn't much she could do about it. Just as I was about to head off to basic training, I discovered that the recruiter I'd seen had made all sorts of promises to me that he wasn't capable of keeping. That was a dealbreaker, so I decided to give the Marines a try.

I told the recruiter there that I wanted to go into aviation.

"Absolutely," he said. "No problem."

I had several other mandatories, and he agreed to all of them.

Within a few days, I was on my way to boot camp in San Diego, California.

Boot camp was hellish, but then I suppose it's meant to be. As I mentioned earlier, I wasn't the biggest, strongest guy in my unit – quite the opposite in fact. But I worked hard completing all the obstacle courses and doing everything the drill instructor asked. I was determined to succeed as a Marine, so I hung in there.

Unfortunately for me, the drill instructor hated me. Yes, I know that drill sergeants aren't supposed to be nice to anyone. They are there to drive their men to the limit – to make fighting soldiers out of them. But my instructor took out all his anger on me. Every day, all day long, I bore the brunt of his physical and verbal abuse. The other guys had nothing to fear when I was around, because I was the lightning rod for the sergeant's bad temper.

How bad was it? Twice during the twelve weeks of basic training, he knocked me unconscious. I never even knew why he attacked me. I would see him coming toward me, his face red with anger, foam flying off his lips as he screamed my name. The next thing I knew, I'd be waking up on the ground, with a terrible headache. I consider myself lucky that he didn't kill me.

What made the situation even worse for me was that the bullying spread, as it often does. When the other recruits saw how the DI was treating me, many of them began picking on me, too. They were bonding by abusing me, making points with the drill instructor and each other at my expense.

This kind of treatment went on for the next three years, until I re-entered civilian life. When I entered the Marines, I had been thinking seriously about a military career. But there was no way I could continue to endure the abuse that had been heaped upon me.

Although my military service had begun at the tail-end of the Vietnam War and I had not seen any fighting, by the time I left the Marines, I felt like I had been through three years of combat. I was suffering from Post-Traumatic Stress Disorder and didn't know where to go for help.

For a period of over a year, I was homeless, spending most of my time on the streets, which wasn't at all easy, especially in the winter in Wisconsin. Sometimes, I was able to stay with a friend for a day or two. Most of the time, I drifted from shelter to shelter. Occasionally, I slept in the back of an old car.

It was also during this time that I sought comfort in drugs and became addicted to crack cocaine. When crack has its claws in you, it's very hard to get free. I was about as low as a person can go.

Of course, it's not easy for me to share some of these things. It's difficult, but I'm not ashamed, because I know that what happened to me could happen to anyone. That's why it's so important to learn how to protect yourself from bullying and abuse.

It would be a huge understatement to say that it wasn't easy for me to get back on my feet. You don't snap out of PTSD in an instant. But basically, my recovery took this path:

1. I discovered that there were people who cared about me and wanted me to succeed. I found many of these people in a 12-step program. There is power in numbers. If you surround yourself with bullies and abusers, they will drag you down. But when you join with people who want to see you succeed, they will lift you up. I understand that we can't always escape from bullies – and, in fact, bullies seem to be everywhere these days. But if there is anything you can do to limit your contact with mean and abusive people, then do it.

2. I became aware that there is a God who loves me and wants the best for me. My faith was instrumental in my recovery and though I have no statistical evidence to back this up, I believe that faith-based recovery programs work better than those that are not faith-based.

3. I changed the way I viewed myself and talked to myself. I realized that I didn't have to believe the cruel words of those who had bullied me. They didn't really know me, so what right did they have to judge me? I reminded myself constantly that "I am somebody" and "I have within myself the potential to do great things." As I did this, I discovered that there is great power in positive self-talk. Any time you are tempted to berate yourself with thoughts such as, "I am so inept. I can't do anything right," make a conscious effort to change your inner dialogue to something like, "I have many talents and abilities. I am capable of doing whatever I put my mind to."

4. I took my eyes off myself. As I started being less concerned about my own predicament, and more concerned about others who had been abused and traumatized, I began to recover. As Gandhi said, "The best way to find yourself is to lose yourself in service to others."

5. I discovered the benefits of hypnotherapy.

Through hypnotherapy, I was able to go into my past and rediscover my dignity and self-confidence. I was able to see that I was picked on, not because of who I am, but because of a total misperception of who I am. The problem was never with me. The problem was with my tormentors. One of the most important things I was able to do with the help of therapy was to go back and forgive those who abused me. Again, it wasn't easy, but I did it. I also forgave myself for not standing up to them any better than I did. In my imagination, I sometimes saw myself sweeping my enemies away as if I were Bruce Lee or Chuck Norris. I could just imagine the surprised looks on their faces when I unleashed a lightning-fast barrage of kung fu moves on them. But that was in my mind. The truth was I was always outnumbered, and unable to fight back, so I had to take what they were dishing out. I had nothing to be ashamed of – and neither do you.

Unforgiveness is a killer. It will tie you up in knots and prevent you from living life to the fullest. Harboring unforgiveness can lead to all kind of emotional and physical problems, like high blood pressure, gastro-intestinal issues, anxiety, depression, headaches and more. It is imperative that we forgive, if not for our enemy's benefit, then for our own.

Hypnotherapy was such a great help to be that I decided to go back to school and become a hypnotherapist myself. I was driven to help others overcome the damage that had been done to them by cruel people and careless parents, and I have been doing it ever since.

MORE WAYS TO FIGHT BACK AGAINST BULLIES

Please don't do what I did and suffer in silence when and if you are picked on and bullied. Bullies are looking for victims, who won't or can't fight back. Here are some ways you can help your kids stand up for themselves.

1. Talk to them about what they are going through Are they having trouble with any particular child or children? If so, why? Is there something practical that can be done about it? I also suggest you also talk to the other child's parents – not in a threatening way – but to see if you can come to a mutual plan to fix the problem. If the bully's parents insist that

their child is an angel who would never ever bully someone, then take the matter to the appropriate teacher, principal, coach, or other adult leader.

2.Whatever you do, please do not get angry. Be forceful, if necessary, but be calm. You should never get personally involved in your child's battles by attacking the other child or children directly. Doing this can get you into serious trouble.

A man I know was outraged when his middle-school-aged daughter came home from school every day with stories about being picked on and taunted by four mean girls. They did things like taking her sweater and throwing it in a tree. They slapped her and pushed her as she waited for the school bus. Finally, at his wits' end and understandably concerned about his daughter's welfare, he phoned all the other girls and told them to leave her alone. He didn't threaten them specifically, but implied that there would be hell to pay if they continued their bullying behavior. The girls went to their parents, who called the police. My acquaintance was arrested on a charge of making terrorist threats and spent the weekend in jail. The lesson is, no matter how justifiably angry you might be, make sure your behavior is above approach.

2)Keep the lines of communication open

Don't think you've done your job by talking to your kids once or twice about bullying. Encourage them to open up about the situation as often as they need to. Make sure they know you are always ready to listen.

3) Try role playing

One good way to prevent bullying is to be prepared for it and plan ahead. Ask your child, "What are you going to do if he does this?" "What are you going to say if he calls you this or that name?" Then, act the situation out with your child, thinking of responses that won't necessarily escalate the situation, but that will, hopefully, get the bully to back off. One of the best approaches is to hold your head up, keep a smile on your face, and don't show your antagonist that he is scaring you or hurting your feelings. No whining or crying. You can't win by expecting a bully to take pity on you.

4) Hold your head up!

Another important thing you can do is help your child develop positive body language. The person who is bullied has won half the battle if he stands up tall and straight and appears not to be fazed when he is called names and insulted in other ways.

Part of teaching your child how to maintain strong, positive body language is encouraging him and helping him build up his confidence. Remind him that it doesn't matter what the bully says, because it's not true. He or she doesn't have to believe it. Tell him, "Maybe he is picking on you because you're smarter than he is – or because you have more friends than he does. He is trying to bring you down because he's jealous of you." It's always important to affirm your child, to remind him of all his good qualities and how proud he makes you feel. But this is especially important when he is getting picked on. This is when he or she needs your encouragement more than ever.

5) Tell your child to report it "Nobody likes a tattle tale."

Most parents have said something like this to their children at one time or another – usually when siblings are fighting about something and telling on each other. In fact, I think this has been said so much that children have come to think that they should never report wrongdoing to the authorities, and that's not true. If a child is being bullied at school, they need to report it to his teacher, principal or people in other positions of authority. Explain to him that you can't be there to see what's going on at school, so it's important to get other adult authorities involved.

Because bullying is such a problem these days, most schools have clear policies on bullying, and your child's teacher should be prepared to intervene. So, if your child is being bullied on the playground, in the restroom, or on the bus, he should report it immediately. Many schools have a zero-tolerance policy for bullying, which is as it should be. If, for some reason, your child attends a school that doesn't know how to deal with bullies, and you can't get any satisfaction from his or her teacher or principal, you may want to bring up the subject at the next school board meeting. If all else fails, you may want to consider moving your child to a private school. It really is that important. Being bullied can scar a child for the rest of their life. And although I don't think you should let a bully force you to change your life, if you have tried everything else, and the bullying persists then it's worth making a major lifestyle change in order to get away from it.

When Melissa was fifteen, she began being bullied by a group of "mean girls" at her school. Their constant attacks on her came out of the blue. It seemed that one day the other girls decided they didn't like her, for whatever reason, and started calling her names and challenging her to fight them – all at once. They began looking for her after school every day and would do things like knock her books out of her hands, tear up her homework papers and call her vulgar and insulting names.

Melissa's parents knew that something was going on, because her grades were dropping, and she often complained of stomachaches and severe headaches that kept her home from school. They hoped it was a phase that would pass, but it didn't. Instead, the situation got so bad that Melissa tried to commit suicide by jumping off a bridge near her home.

Melissa didn't die, but she did break both of her ankles and had to miss school for several weeks. It was during that time that her parents discovered the full story of what was going on at school. Even though it was difficult financially for them to do so, when Melissa recovered, they put her in a private school. Today, she's doing well, on schedule to graduate with her class, and there has been no more bullying.

I'm telling you Melissa's story because it illustrates that drastic measures are sometimes necessary.

You may be wondering, "What about the bullies? Are they still getting away with their behavior?"

Unfortunately, probably so. The school gave them a slap on the wrist, hinted that Melissa was partly to blame for the situation (even though the "mean girls" had a history of harassing other kids, and did nothing else. Unfortunately, things don't always turn out the way you want them to. But the important thing is that Melissa is no longer being mistreated, and the school has received her complaint about the conduct of the bullies.

FOOD FOR THOUGHT

- We advised you to do your best to avoid contact with mean and abusive people. What can you or your children do to follow through on this recommendation?
- One of the best ways you can find yourself is to lose yourself in service to others. Can you think of some ways you can use your natural gifts and abilities to help others?
- Unforgiveness is a killer. It will tie you in knots and prevent you from living life to the fullest – so forgive yourself and others. Is there someone you especially need to forgive right now?

Remember:

- If your child is being bullied, talk to him about what he's going through and keep the lines of communication open.
- Hold your head up and know in advance how you will respond to any situation.
- There is power in positive self-talk, so use it – especially when you are tempted to put yourself down.

PART THREE
THE (NOT-SO)
ROARING TWENTIES

CHAPTER FIVE

STILL STRUGGLING AFTER ALL THESE YEARS?

According to our society, when a person reaches his 21st birthday, he or she is no longer a child, but an adult. Sadly, nothing magical happens on that day to suddenly set that newly minted 21-year-old free from the trouble and strife that childhood brings. They don't suddenly become a mature adult, capable of making wise decisions, holding down a job, paying the bills, and handling all the troubles life can bring. Some 21-yearolds are quite capable of making it on their own, but many more of them are not.

In fact, in these days when more children are living with their parents until their mid20s, or even longer, twenty-somethings are facing more problems than ever before. If you are struggling to help your twenty-something child become a mature adult, you are not alone. You have plenty of company.

But don't blame yourself, because it's most likely not your fault. Nor is it your child's fault. Mostly, I think the problem has to do with this fast-paced, high-pressure world we live in. But that doesn't mean there's nothing we can do to remedy the situation.

Before we get into some of the specific problems faced by twenty-somethings, let me say that it is not necessarily a bad thing that many young people are taking longer to find themselves. For example, it's good that people are waiting a bit longer to marry, instead of rushing to the altar in haste, and then having to repent at leisure. More about this later.

In their book, *Not Quite Adults*, Richard Settersten, PhD, and Barbara E. Ray contend that the fact that twenty-somethings are taking a slower path to adulthood is "good for everyone." Based on 10 years of research and more than 500 interviews, the authors refute the notion that today's young people are immature and have a highly developed sense of their own entitlement.6 Instead, they say that young adults who delay marriage and child-rearing get a much better start in life – and that most twenty-somethings who live at home are doing so in order to gain necessary credentials and save money for a more secure future.

They also contend that, "Helicopter parents aren't so bad after all. Involved parents provide young people with advantages, including mentoring and economic support, that have become increasingly necessary to success." 7

And so, it's true that many of what the world sees as problems may not be problems at all. In a world where there are so many real issues that need our attention, we mustn't waste our time looking for issues where there are none. Having said that, let's look at some "real issues."

THE QUARTER-LIFE CRISIS

Just about everyone has heard of a mid-life crisis, the time when a person who is around fifty years of age suddenly goes off the rails and tries to reclaim his youth. He's been a solid, dependable citizen for many years, and he suddenly quits his job, buys a backpack, and heads off to travel the world. Or he may spend all his money on a flashy red sports car. It sounds comical, but a midlife crisis can be extremely damaging to the "victim" and his or her family.

But have you ever heard of a "quarter-life crisis?" They call it a quarter-life crisis because it affects people who are in their twenties – at about a quarter of the average person's life span. It is also known as a crisis of confidence, and many mental health professionals will tell you that it's even worse than the better-known mid-life crisis.

What causes a quarter-life crisis?

Many things.

It often comes with the realization that life is about to change forever, and you've got to get ready to handle it. For example, suppose you're starting your junior year in college. The first two years have been full of parties and fun. Everything has been great. Then it hits you. "In two more years, I'm out of this place. I'll be on my own. I'll need a good job. I'll have to pay my own bills. But what happens if I can't find a job? What will I do? Where will I go?" The panic gets worse when you realize that you'll walk out of school with something like $40,000 of student loan debt hanging over you.

As you think about all that, you may start wondering if you'll be able to finish college at all. After all, your classes are getting harder, and you just read the statistic that only 40 percent of college freshmen make it all the way through to graduation.

Some people have a quarter-life crisis because they feel that they are faking it – that everyone expects them to behave like grownups, but they "know" deep down inside they are still children. They fear they are frauds, and they are about to be exposed.

Others are not ready for the happy, fun-filled years of college to end. They feel that the best is over, and it's all downhill from here.

Another reason why people experience a quarter-life crisis is that they feel they have far too many decisions to make, and they become paralyzed by fear and inertia. Some of them have never had much practice making their own decisions, because their parents have always told them what to do. They want to be free to live life their way, but they don't quite know how to do it.

When a person is in his twenties, he or she is expected to be strong, good-looking, fit, smart, hip, and ambitious. That's a lot of pressure. By the time they reach their 40s, most people don't care about such things with the intensity they felt when they were fresh out of college. Sadly, most people who are going through a crisis of confidence don't get much sympathy from their parents or older people in general. As is the case with our childhoods, when most of us look back at our twenties, we see them through a rosy glow.

"Ah, how wonderful to be young again!" We think it was great fun choosing a career, looking for a lifetime companion, deciding where we wanted to live and what we wanted to do with our lives — but we forget how terrifying it all could be.

How do you deal with a quarter-life crisis?

Let me repeat something I've said several times before. If the problem is severe and you can't seem to beat it on your own, then start looking for a good therapist. But you can also:

1) Find peace through volunteering

One of the best ways to overcome depression, sadness and worry is to reach out to others. I've had clients who were offended when I told them they could find relief by taking their eyes off themselves and thinking about others. They seemed to think that I was telling them, "Your problem is that you're too selfish. Stop thinking about yourself and you'll feel better." But selfishness is not the problem. It's natural to be focused on yourself when you're going through a bad time. But the more you dwell on your own issues, the bigger they will seem to you. When you start helping other people with their problems, your own issues may seem smaller. (Please note that when I talk about dwelling on your issues, I'm not talking about problem solving. It's a good thing to spend time thinking of solutions to your problems, but it is not a good thing to spend time brooding about the situation.)

There are dozens of good organizations that count on help from volunteers. A few of them are:

- Big Brothers and Big Sisters
- Boys and Girls Clubs
- Boy Scouts and Girl Scouts
- Meals on Wheels
- Little League
- Food Banks
- A Hospital Auxiliary
- Rescue Missions

And the list goes on and on.

2) Get involved in something bigger than yourself.

Another way to climb out of a quarter-life crisis is to get involved with a group of people who are working toward a common goal. There is something exhilarating and uplifting about being part of something bigger than yourself. It can be a source of power and joy.

Some of the organizations mentioned above provide wonderful opportunities to do this. For example, if you get involved with an organization like Big Brothers and Big Sisters, you are taking two steps toward recovery. First, you are getting your mind off yourself by helping others. Second, you are joining with others in reaching toward a common goal – in this case giving young men and women a role model, and the guidance they need to succeed in school and in life. Being a part of something greater than yourself will give you an understanding of the intrinsic value of human life. Your life has meaning, and you can find it by joining hands with others in the pursuit of a common goal.

As the late Norman Vincent Peale said, "The more you lose yourself in something greater than yourself, the more energy you will have."

3) Find a mentor

One of the reasons why people fall into a quarter-life crisis is that they are afraid of what the future will bring. They feel stuck and don't know how to get unstuck. One of the best ways of moving forward is to find a good mentor to give you the benefit of his or her wisdom and experience. A mentor is not someone who will tell you what to do, or who will make decisions for you. Rather, he or she can help you make the right decisions and serve as a sounding-board for you. A mentor can help you grow personally and professionally. Many of the most successful people I know have mentors – or serve as mentors.

Once you've made up your mind that you want to have a mentor, how do you choose one? Your mentor should be:

Someone you trust completely. Can you trust this person to keep your confidential conversations confidential? Are you convinced that he or she has your best interest at heart? You certainly don't want to have a mentor who will share your secrets with others.

Someone you admire. This is common sense. Why would you ask someone to mentor you if you don't admire them? But what I mean is please don't choose someone just because he has been successful in his career. It's important for your mentor to be someone you genuinely like and feel comfortable with. Before you ask someone to mentor you, take the time to observe him and see how he treats other people and how he behaves in all situations. Don't choose someone who is condescending or critical.

A success in the path you've chosen.

Here's another a piece of advice based on common sense. You don't want to ask someone to mentor you just because he or she is a nice person. Your mentor must be someone who has proved themselves capable in the field you want to go into.

You want someone who can tell you from his own experiences how to succeed in your chosen path. He should be someone who can tell you how to open doors, or take the necessary steps you need to take to get headed to move in right direction. He may not be able to answer all your questions, but he should be able to tell you how to go about finding the answers you need.

Someone who is dependable.

Mentoring someone is a huge responsibility. It takes time, and dedication. A mentor must be willing to meet with you on a regular basis. You have to know that they are going to be there when you've planned – that they won't blow you off because something else came up or forget that the two of you had a meeting scheduled. I realize you really can't know if someone is dependable until you start working with them, but you can have a pretty good idea by observing how he relates to others. And if you start working with someone and find out that they're not really dependable, tell him it's not working out and start searching for another mentor.

Someone who is truly interested in working with you.

You won't really know if this is the case until you ask someone if they are willing to work with you. But at that point, if you sense more than a little hesitation, I suggest that you find someone else. Understand that a little reluctance is to be expected, especially if the person you ask has never been a mentor before. It's a big commitment, and your prospective mentor may wonder, at first, if they are really up to the challenge. But you can usually tell whether his reluctance is based on nervousness about letting you down, or if he simply doesn't want to do it. If he really doesn't want to do it, find someone else.

Where do you find a mentor?

The answer is, just about anywhere. They may be a teacher, coach or professor at your school, a leader in your church, a co-worker or fellow student, a neighbor, someone you've met at your gym, a favorite aunt or uncle, and so on. Keep your eyes open, and don't write anyone off. And don't think that your mentor has to be someone on a "higher level" than you. They may be someone who is your peer – who has the same amount of experience as you – but who has some particular skills you would like to emulate.

There are also a number of good books and online articles that can tell you more about how to find a good mentor and get the most out of a mentoring relationship. If you are feeling stuck in neutral and looking for a way to get your life into gear, check them out.

4) Look for an internship

Sometimes, twenty-somethings go into a quarter-life crisis because they can't find a job right away after graduation from college. This is actually a cyclical situation. Some years the economy is booming and there are plenty of jobs. Other years, the economy is struggling and nobody's hiring. Some years, there are plenty of jobs in a particular field. Then, the next year, all the jobs are in another field.

Admittedly, it can be nerve-wracking to be unemployed, especially when you're looking for your first-ever real job. But here's one thing you can do if you can't find a job in your field: Look for an internship. Many companies offer internships to college students and recent graduates. An internship is a great way to get your foot in the door and show what you can do. It is true that most internships don't pay, although some do. But you should consider it an investment in your future. And, at this time in your life, the experience you receive might be more valuable than money. You can check for internships by searching the websites of companies you would like to work for or by checking in with their human resources departments, especially with the person who handles recruiting. There are also a number of websites to help you, and Huffington Post says the following are four of the best.

Internships.com

This website allows you to search for internships by major, job category, location, and company. It also lets you know whether you will be paid or get other benefits, like college credit — and provides resources such as internship basics, an intern stories blog, and tips for better interviews. Huffington Post says, "Be sure to check out the Internship Predictor®, a tool that uses your personal preferences and personality to help you find current opportunities that will be the best fit for you!"

- **Idealist.org**
- This website is designed especially for people who are looking for an internship in the nonprofit world. You'll be able to find internships by their area of focus, whether they're paid or unpaid, and even by language! Each internship listing includes a job description, instructions for how to apply, and other valuable information.
- **Experience.com**
- Huffington Post says that this website is a winner because of its connection to colleges and universities. "Many educational institutions, including Duke University, the University of Tampa, Spelman College, and DePaul University, use Experience.com as a

platform for students in their career centers to find internships, and new listings are added to the site every day." This website will also let you know about job fairs that are happening in your area. Be aware that you must register and become a member of this website in order to use it to apply for jobs.

- **Mediabistro.com**
- Looking for an internship in the media? Mediabistro is the way to go. It has the largest job board in the United States for media professionals, including jobs in social media.

Huffington Post says, "The easiest way to search on Mediabistro is to filter to internships specifically. So many media positions are listed that if you do not take advantage of that filter first, you'll have to do extraneous searching, taking up time you could be using to apply for other internships!"

FOOD FOR THOUGHT

- According to some researchers, young people who delay marrying and rearing children get off to a better start in life. Do you think this is true? Why or why not?
- Can you name three things you can do to overcome a quarter-life crisis?
- Find peace through volunteerism
- Get involved in something bigger than yourself
- Find a mentor to help you find navigate your way to success
- Could you use the services of a reliable mentor? If so, start drawing up a list of those you could ask to mentor you.

Remember:

- Some people in their twenties go through a debilitating experience known as a "quarter-life crisis" or "a crisis of confidence." Such a crisis may be triggered by the realization that a young person is about to be responsible for his own life and welfare.

---

6 Richard A. Settersten & Barbara E. Ray, "Not Quite Adults: Why 20-somethings are Choosing a Slower Path to Adulthood, and Why It's Good for Everyone," (Bantam Books: New York) 2010

7 Not Quite Adults, Page XV

CHAPTER SIX
BEWARE THE LIES OF SOCIAL MEDIA

There are many other reasons why young people go through a crisis of confidence. Some of these reasons are obvious, while others aren't clear at all. Social media is one that may surprise you, but therapists are seeing more and more people who have become distressed and depressed due to their involvement in Facebook, Twitter, Instagram, Snapchat and other forms of social media.

There seems to be a natural law that every new invention that comes into the world to make our lives better can also be used to make us miserable.

 e airplane gave us the ability to travel long distances in a short time, but within two decades of Orville and Wilbur Wright's first flight, airplanes were being used to drop bombs from the sky.

Nuclear power can provide an abundant supply of relatively low-cost energy. But it can also be used for weapons that have the potential to destroy us all.

Opioids can provide relief from debilitating pain but have killed thousands of people who abused them.

I'm sure you can think of many similar examples.

The same is true of the internet — and social media in particular. Thanks to the internet, a few clicks on a keyboard can bring us an entire world full of vital information. The internet allows us to communicate with other people all over the world – but it also opens us up to bullies and causes us to pretend to be what we're not.

As if you didn't already know this, social media platforms like Facebook are filled with lies told by people who want others to think their lives are better than they really are. Facebook is a lot like Garrison Keillor's Lake Wobegon, a place where "All the women are strong, all the men are good looking, and all the children are above average." On social media, everybody has a good job and goes on expensive vacations. Every child gets good grades and excels on the sports field. There are no hum-drum run-of-the mill lives here.

Why is that a problem? Because it turns out that peer pressure is a serious issue, not only in the middle school years, but throughout life. It is the old predicament of messing up your life by trying to keep up with the Joneses. Of course, we shouldn't care about what other people have, or begrudge them their successes – but we do.

In her book, *The Happiness Effect: How Social Media is Driving a Generation to Appear Perfect at Any Cost*, Donna Freitas writes, "In our attempts to be happy, to distract ourselves from our deeper, sometimes darker thoughts, we experience the opposite effect. In trying to always appear happy, we rob ourselves of joy. . . I worry that social media is teaching us that we are not worthy. That it has us living in a compulsive and perpetual loop of such feedback. That in our constant attempts to edit out our imperfections for massive public viewing, we are losing sight of the things that ground our life in connection and love, in meaning and relationships.

"Our brave faces are draining us. We're losing sight of our authentic selves."[8]

Just this morning, as I turned on my laptop to begin writing, I saw a news story about a popular online "influencer" who had been sending out videos and texts that were supposedly from her luxury hotel in Bali. Only she wasn't in Bali. She was in her neighborhood Ikea store. This is a case in point of someone trying to make herself look more important and successful than she really is.

Freitas writes about a young woman named Margaret, one of many college students she interviewed who told her they are often troubled by what they read on social media. Margaret says, "I'm not really as involved on

Facebook because I compare myself to a lot of other people, and Facebook is a really easy way to do that. You can just click on other people's posts, see everything that everyone's doing, and when I see that on Facebook, I think, 'Oh, they're all doing that, they're just so happy.'"

As a result, Margaret feels as if she's missing out, that her life isn't as good as the life her peers are living: "I forget about all the great things that are happening in my life, that I need to notice," she says. "It's just been an easy trap for me to get into, just comparing myself, and Facebook does not help."[9]

Does this mean that Facebook and other social media platforms are inherently evil? Of course not. It's just that you always have to consider the source and take what you read and see with a large grain of salt.

Freitas writes that when Margaret was on Facebook more often, she tended to grade herself by the number of likes her posts got, in comparison to the number of likes other people's posts received. Not getting enough likes made her feel that she wasn't as popular as she wanted to be — or wasn't hanging out with the right people.

"You can do a lot of damage on Facebook," Margaret says. "Like, I was never bullied on Facebook, or anything, but to be honest I've always sort of bullied myself. I put myself down on a lot of things and judge myself really critically."[10]

How can you deal with the pressures that social media puts on you? The best thing you can do is to try to stop competing and just be yourself. Understand that the person you are is good enough, strong enough, and you don't have to pretend to be someone you're not. Remember that it doesn't matter how many likes you get. The only people who are liked by everyone are those who never stand up for anything.

If you can't stop competing, and if social media makes you feel bad about yourself, then stop using it. Yes, I know that's easier said than done. You may not be able to quit cold turkey – but you can do it with hard work and perseverance. That's what Michael did.

There was a time when Michael₁₁ was a devoted fan of social media. But as he got older, he became more and more convinced that it was all about competition and making oneself look as good as possible. His dissatisfaction came to a head when he went with a group of friends to a baseball game. The whole thing turned out to be staged for the benefit of Facebook. It was choreographed, like a Hollywood musical. Michael and his friends literally spent hours performing for the cameras.

"Okay, everybody, put your arms up in the air and smile!"

"Lean in together and look at the scorecard, like you see something that's really funny and exciting!"

In between staged photos, the girls refreshed their makeup, brushed their hair and did everything they could to look their best for the photographer.

Everything seemed to be fake. And so much time was spent making it look like they were having a good time that they didn't really enjoy the game at all.

A few weeks later, Michael closed his Facebook account.

Does he miss it? In some ways. But he feels a lot better about himself now that he's no longer "addicted" to social media or self-promotion.

Now, please remember that when we started this chapter together, I said that social media is a good thing. There is nothing inherently wrong with Facebook, Twitter, Instagram, or most of the rest of it. It is a tool for staying connected with people we care about. But when it becomes a means for self-promotion, or becomes a means for competing with others, then it might be time to reconsider your involvement.

FOOD FOR THOUGHT

- In this chapter, we said that social media is both good and bad. Do you believe that social media's benefits outweigh its drawbacks, or the other way around? Will this affect the way you use social media, and if so, how?
- Do you agree or disagree with Donna Freitas, who writes, "I worry that social media is teaching us that we are not worthy? That it has us living in a compulsive and perpetual loop of such feedback. That in our constant attempts to edit out our imperfections for massive public viewing, we are losing sight of the things that ground our life in connection and love, in meaning and relationships." •In your estimation, how does social media make our lives easier?
- How do you think social media makes our lives harder?

Remember:

- Nobody is forcing you to use social media. If you can't stop competing, and it makes you feel bad, it may be time to log off.

Freitas, Donna, "The Happiness Effect," (London: Oxford University Press) 2017, Pages XV!-XVII

Freitas, Page 19

Frietas, Pages 18-19

Freitas, Pages 20-23

CHAPTER SEVEN
LEARNING TO MAKE THE RIGHT DECISION

During our twenties, we must make dozens of decisions that will impact the rest of our lives. Making the right decision can prevent years of heartache and grief. For example, will you decide to stay completely away from drugs?

There was a time when drugs were more of a "high-school" thing. And it is true that many American high-schoolers are still struggling with addiction. But I am seeing more young people who made it safely through the teen years, only to stumble in their twenties. Over the last few years, we have seen an increasing number of deaths due to heroin overdoses. According to the Centers for Disease Control, in 2017, nearly 500,000 Americans reported using heroin at least once in the previous year. This represents a 500 percent increase since 2010. Some 15,000 Americans died of heroin overdoses in the same year.[12]

Even though that is a huge number, it really amounts to a very small percentage of drug deaths. Overall, there were 70,000 fatal drug overdoses in 2017 – the last year for which records are available – and 68 percent of them were caused by abuse of prescription drugs – especially opioids. Now, 70,000 deaths in one year works out to more than 191 every day, or just under eight every hour. It is also nearly twice the number of people who are killed by auto accidents in the United States each year.

Add to this the destruction that is being caused by crystal meth and new drugs like fentanyl – and you are looking at a very dangerous landscape.

Before I get further into the subject, let me tell you, again, that this is one subject where I know from personal experience what I'm talking about. I've already shared about my time as a Marine, and how I wound up living on the streets after my discharge.

I hadn't been out of the service for very long when an acquaintance of mine — a fellow Marine – introduced me to crack cocaine. He insisted it would make me forget all my troubles and feel good – and I wanted to feel good. What I didn't know was that I would also be addicted – almost instantly.

My desire for crack cocaine took over my life. It robbed me of my money and my ambition. My dependence on cocaine was the primary reason that I wound up living on the streets. I went through rehab four times, and four times I relapsed within weeks of "graduation."

For me, the change began when I took my eyes off myself and started to care about others. In fact, my desire for cocaine seemed to diminish proportionately to my growing concern for others.

One of the turning points for me came when I was sitting in a crack house, and saw a young man collapse, and nearly die, after smoking fentanyl. He took a hit and I saw his eyes roll back in his head, and then he fell backwards against the wall. I thought he was dead – but quick action saved his life.

He was very lucky. Fentanyl is an extremely dangerous drug that has been responsible for thousands of deaths over the past few years. But what I had seen shocked me and made my heart go out to him. People were losing their futures and lives to drugs and someone needed to help them. I decided to be the one to do that and, with great effort, began the process that enabled me to leave my drug addiction behind.

From this, I learned that the very best way to help yourself is to help others. I know that this seems counter-intuitive. But it is precisely when you get your eyes off your own troubles that they begin to disappear. Does it seem to you that I keep coming back to this topic? That's because it is so very important!

We'll talk more about this in just a bit. But first, I must say that if you, or your child, is having a problem with drugs, please get professional help right away. And, because people with drug addictions often find it difficult to admit it, I urge you to face up to the truth.

Whenever I hear someone say, "I'm not hooked. I can quit any time I want to," I know he's lying to himself. It's only when you admit you need help that you can ask for it. And unless you ask for it, you're not likely to get it. Are drugs a problem for you or someone you love? Here are 10 ways you can figure it out:

HOW TO TELL IF YOU MIGHT BE ADDICTED

You keep taking a drug even when you no longer need it for medical reasons.

You need to take an increasingly large amount of the drug before it has any effect on you.

You feel shaky, queasy, tired or hungry when you run out of the drug.

You keep using a drug even though it's causing you to have trouble with friends, family, work, or the law.

When you're not actually using the drug, you are consumed by thoughts about the drug or how good it makes you feel.

You've lost interest in things you were once passionate about – such as music, sports, or relationships.

You borrow or steal – even from your own friends or family — to buy drugs.

Your friends and family keep asking you if something is wrong or talking about how you've changed.

There are many more signs, of course, but these are some of the major ones. If you recognize yourself or your loved one in any of these, don't wait and hope that things will get better over time. Get help now!

Whether or not to take drugs is one of the life-changing decisions that most young people have to make. Really, it should be a no-brainer. Taking recreational drugs of any kind is dangerous. Abstaining from drugs is beneficial. But there are many other decisions that are not so obvious. They don't seem dangerous, but that they are. Some people spend their lives in misery because the married the wrong person or chose the wrong career:

DON'T GET MARRIED FOR THE WRONG REASON

This is also the time of life when most people choose a mate. Sadly, when you're in your twenties, you're likely to do it for the wrong reasons. Did you know that 41 percent of all first marriages end in divorce, and it gets worse for those who remarry? Some 60 percent of second marriages break up, and 73 per cent of third marriages end in divorce. Apparently, people don't get smarter and easier to live with as time goes by. Having said

that, it is true that the younger you are when you marry for the first time, the more likely you are to get divorced.

Do not marry a young lady because she has a nice figure or a sexy smile.

Do not marry a young man because he's a star on the football team or is a sharp dresser.

Don't marry someone because he or she is a good kisser or a terrific dancer.

All of these reasons are extremely superficial and are likely to change over time. For example, if you think you're in love with a girl because she has a sexy figure, how are you going to feel when she's gained 15 or 20 pounds? Or if you choose a husband because he's an athlete, what's going to happen ten years down the road when his glory days are behind him and he's gotten paunchy around the middle?

Obviously, this is not a book about finding the right mate, or how to stay happy in a marriage. There are plenty of good books on these subjects, and you can find them at any library. But I also feel that it's important for me to touch on the subject, because so many young adults mess up their lives by choosing a partner for the wrong reasons.

One of the worst – and it's one that I hear again and again – is emotional blackmail.

"He said that he would kill himself if I left him. What could I do?"

"She said that I had to marry her because I took her virginity. She said nobody else would want her. It was my duty to marry her."

The person who threatens suicide before marriage is likely to do it again and again after marriage. The person who marries someone else out of "duty" is likely to resent it for the rest of his or her life.

I am not condoning promiscuous behavior, but the plain truth is that mistakes happen. If you feel that you have wronged someone, apologize for it and let it go. If you think a suicide threat should be taken seriously, report it to a clergyman or other authority. If you feel a suicide attempt is imminent, either call 911 or a suicide hotline if there is one in your community. You can also call the National Suicide Prevention Lifeline at 800 273-8255.

DON'T CHOOSE A CAREER FOR THE WRONG REASON

Marriage is a life-time commitment, so think very carefully about what you're doing. Pay attention to warning signs. Don't make the mistake of thinking that he will get his temper under control, or that she'll cut back on her drinking.

You definitely don't want to spend the next 50 years of your life married to someone who makes you miserable. The same is true of your career. How terribly sad to spend decades of your life in a job that feels like drudgery. Once again, I am a case in point. It was not until I was in my 30s that I discovered the fulfillment that comes through helping others as a hypnotherapist.

I know many people who changed their careers after realizing they had made choices when they were younger that were not well-suited to their temperaments, personalities or skill sets. I also know many people who are happily employed in jobs that have nothing to do with the degrees they earned or courses of study they took in college. One man got a degree in chemical engineering, and he spent 20 years working in that profession. He was smart and did well. But he was also miserable. His hobby was carpentry and he loved working with his hands. He figured out a way to turn his hobby into a full-time career, and he loves it. He doesn't make as much money as he did before – but he's much happier.

What are some of the wrong reasons for choosing a job?

Because it pays well.

Because it's prestigious.

Because it's what your family or friends expect of you.

Because you're not sure what else to do.

Because there seem to be a lot of job openings in this field.

I admit that these are not necessarily bad reasons. There is some merit in each of them, so long as it is not your primary reason for choosing a career. For example, the fact that there are a lot of job openings in a certain field can be a significant reason for pursuing a career in that field, so long as it's something that you also have an aptitude for, and something that you would enjoy doing.

For example, one young man I know decided to pursue a career as a speech therapist, after his research told him that the field was dominated by women. He figured, correctly, that being a member of a small minority would open doors for him. He was more likely to be accepted into the college he wanted. He was more likely to receive scholarships and other financial aid. And after graduation, he would be attractive to prospective employers who were looking to diversify their staffs.

Certainly, all these things seemed to be true, and he has had a very successful career, now overseeing a staff of nearly 100 employees. Of course, this isn't all because of his gender. He also happens to have a natural love of people, an empathy that helps him perform his job well. He's smart, hard-working and dedicated to his profession. All of these traits went together to make this career a perfect fit for him.

FOOD FOR THOUGHT

- Can you name five ways to tell if you or someone you love is addicted to drugs? **You keep taking a drug** even when you no longer need it.
- **You need to take** an increasingly large amount before it has any effect on you **You feel shaky**, queasy, tired or hungry when you run out of the drug.
- **You keep using a drug** even though it's causing you to have trouble with friends, family, work, or the law.
- **When you're not actually using** the drug, you are consumed by thoughts about how good it makes you feel.
- **What is the best way** to help yourself get out of trouble?
- **How do we help ourselves** when we help others?

Remember:

- **People who are happiest** in their careers are those who are doing something they love. How can this apply to you?

---

[12] Statistics from U.S. Centers for Disease Control website

CHAPTER EIGHT
THE IMPORTANCE OF SETTING GOALS

Have you ever heard it said that if you don't know where you're going, any road will take you there? The problem is that it probably won't be where you want to go.

You can't just drift through life. By the time you reach your twenties, you need to have a clear idea of where you want to go and how to get there. That doesn't mean you won't come to a fork in the road and change the course you're on. It's perfectly okay to re-triangulate your position. But you must have goals to guide you along your way.

Thomas Edison tried, and failed, to invent the incandescent light bulb some 10,000 times before he finally succeeded. Most people would have given up long before they had failed 100 times. Think about how many failures 10,000 really is. That's an average of five failures a day for more than five years!

But when someone asked the great inventor if he was tempted to give up, he said no. He was excited that he had found 10,000 ways not to invent a light bulb. This is how success comes to scientists and inventors. They change one variable at a time until they find the combination that works. Slowly, surely, the puzzle comes together, and the world is changed.

It is because the inventor has a plan that he is ultimately able to achieve success. His plan must be refined and restructured as he goes along, but it is the planning itself that helps him achieve his goal. What are goals?

Goals *are* real, specific and measurable steps you can take to achieve your dreams.

Goal-setting begins with taking a look at the big picture of your life and asking yourself, "Where do I want to be ten years from now? Five years from now? In one year?"

We all know people who have worked hard for many years, but never seemed to get anywhere. They were just stuck in the same unfulfilling job. They were competent. Reliable. Smart. But they are still pretty much where they started.

What happened? For many, the biggest problem was that they failed to set practical, achievable goals. They didn't have a clearly defined plan to reach a specific destination, so they just drifted from day to day and year to year.

Before you can set realistic goals for your life, you must know where it is you want to go. What is your over-all objective? Suppose you were planning to drive up the Pacific Coast from California to Alaska. Before you made the drive, you'd want to get a good map and figure out how far you'd be able to drive each day. You would also want to know what the conditions of the roads were, where you could get gas and food, etc. Reaching those towns and cities along your route would be the goals that would help you reach your over-all objective.

Whatever your over-all objective may be, your goals are the smaller steps that can help you get there. To be effective, goals must:

Be written

It's important to write your goals as clearly and concisely as possible. If you have trouble writing your goals in a simple, clear sentence, then you probably need to spend more time making sure you have them clear in your own mind.

Be specific and measurable

A goal must be specific so you will be able to measure your progress toward its fulfillment. It can't be nebulous or have too many moving parts. It must be clear enough so that you can know for certain when you achieve it.

Have a deadline attached

I have known people who did a great job of setting goals, but never accomplished any of them. Why not? Because they didn't have a specific deadline attached to them, so they just kept pushing them back in time. Writing down your goals doesn't help you at all if you're not going to take steps to turn them into reality, and having a deadline attached applies the pressure you need to get started. Admittedly, you may find that the deadline you gave yourself is unrealistic. If so, it's okay to change your deadline. But only do this if it is necessary. In other words, don't make a habit out of it. If you are casual in your attitude toward deadlines, they won't have the desired effect. I saw a coffee mug that said, "Deadlines amuse me." It made me smile, but it's not an attitude I'd recommend.

Be realistic

If you can't carry a tune in a bucket, it would be silly to have the goal of becoming a Broadway singer. If you've never been very good at sports, it's not a good idea to set a goal of being a star in the NBA. Your goals must be in line with what you know of your own capabilities and skills. Yes, it is important to stretch yourself, to reach for the stars, as they say. But if you set goals that are entirely beyond your reach you are only going to wind up frustrated and exasperated.

Your goals will change as your experience and circumstances change. Fine-tuning and revising is an important part of the process. Everyone runs into unexpected obstacles. When that happens, take the time to reevaluate and revise your goals accordingly.

As goals are achieved, they must be replaced with new, perhaps higher goals. Remember that having realistic, attainable goals can help you get to where you want to be in life.

FOOD FOR THOUGHT

- **What are goals?**

Goals *are* real, specific and measurable steps you can take to achieve your dreams.

- **Why are goals so important?**

Goals are important because they can move you in the direction of your dreams, one step at a time.

- **Can you name four characteristics of workable goals?**

They are written down

They are specific and measurable

They must have a deadline attached

They must be realistic

- **Why is it so important to write down your goals?**

In order to work, your goals must be as clear and simple as possible. Writing them down helps you cut out the clutter and be more precise.

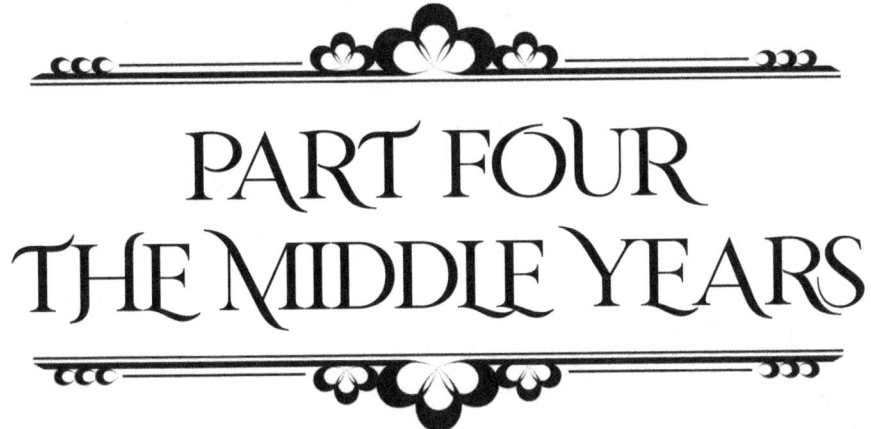

PART FOUR
THE MIDDLE YEARS

CHAPTER NINE

THE THIRTIES: TIME TO TAKE STOCK

For most people, the thirties are good years. This is a time when you have put the turmoil of the twenties behind you. You've settled into a career and are beginning to climb the ladder to the top. Most thirty-somethings are married with children, or are, at least beginning to plan for a family.

When you're in your thirties, you're grown up, but you're still young. In fact, thirty is younger than it has ever been. Today's thirty-year-olds are stronger, healthier and more active than their predecessors. This is in large part due to what we now know about healthy nutrition, fitness, and breakthroughs in medicine. Sometimes, when I see old photographs, from the fifties or earlier, of people who were in their thirties, I'm shocked. They look so old – ten to fifteen years older than I would expect a thirty-something to look today. I understand that I am speaking in broad generalities, and that there are exceptions to every rule. From what I've said so far, the thirties sound like a wonderful time of life for everyone, but that isn't the case.

For some, this time of life is filled with disappointment and dissatisfaction. They tell themselves, "I thought I was going to be happy by now, but I'm not. What did I do wrong?" For these people – and everyone really – the thirties should be a time of taking stock, of figuring out if you're on the right path in life or if some big changes are called for. To do this, you need to step back, take a deep breath and get away for a while – maybe even for a few days – to consider whether you are living the life you always wanted.

WHAT ABOUT YOUR CAREER?

One of the most important questions to ask at this time is, "Am I satisfied with my career?" Do you enjoy what you're doing, or do you often feel like a drudge, little more than a tiny gear in a huge machine? Ask yourself if your job is boring, or if you feel like your creativity and intelligence is being stifled. Does your employer offer a clear path to advancement? Would you even want to have a higher position in your company?

After taking a thorough look at the situation, you may decide that your current career is exactly what you would choose if you could do it all over again. If so, wonderful! But if not, think about what you really want to do and what steps you could take to change things. Perhaps you'll decide to go to graduate school and pursue a degree in a field that appeals to you. Or, you may want to start working with a career counselor who can help you begin searching for a suitable career. It can also be helpful to talk to other people about their careers, finding out what they like most about what they do.

WHAT ABOUT YOUR MARRIAGE?

I need to say right up front, that I do not believe that divorce is the answer to every problem in a marriage. Divorce is a terrible thing that can inflict intense pain on all involved. It is also true that every marriage hits some rough spots now and then. When that happens, I believe in marriage counseling over divorce. But what if you have come to realize that you married the wrong person, and that your life together is a terrible mistake?

I would still suggest that you start off by working with a marriage counselor or your clergyman to see if you can rediscover the love that brought you together in the first place. But if that doesn't work for you, don't stay together "for the sake of the children," because it is not good for any child to be reared in a toxic environment.

This is a very difficult subject, and I don't want you to think that I don't believe in the sanctity and permanence of marriage. I do!

However, there are times when it is best to end a marriage and start over. This should only happen after a great deal of thought and input from a professional counselor or pastor. **CHILDREN VERSUS CAREER**

The thirties is also a time when many people start thinking about having a family. Right now, the average age of a first-time mother in the United States is 28. But a couple of decades ago, the age was 23 – and it seems to be getting later all the time. In fact, the average age of a first-time mother who has a college degree is a bit over 30.

The fact that people are waiting until later to have babies is not a bad thing. First-time parents who are in their 30s may be more mature because of those few extra years of life experiences. They are likely to have more money to spend on their children, and according to a report from the U.S. Department of Agriculture, it costs just under $250,000 to raise a child from birth up to the age of 18. And after that, there's college staring you in the face. Older parents may also have more time to spend with their children as the pressures of the twenties subside.

When it comes to having children, there are two major concerns for women:

1) **Can I continue with my career and raise children?** This is an especially tough question for women who love their careers, or who are beginning to move up at work, and don't want to lose the progress they've made.

2) **How much time do I have left to have children?** Although we are hearing more stories about women having children in their 40s, and even later, these are not common, and there are dangers to both the child and mother. You can't always wait to have a family. The biological clock is ticking, and by the time a woman is in her mid30s, the ticking is quite loud!

How do you know if it's time for you to start a family? Consider these questions:

- **Is your marriage stable?** Can it withstand the new pressures that childhood brings? Being a parent is a wonderful thing, but it is also full of challenges like sleepless nights, dirty diapers, and loud crying – and those are only the beginning.

- **Are you and your spouse on the same page when it comes to starting a family?** Are you both ready to have children? The two of you should agree that this is what you want.

- **How much do you know about raising children?** Have you read books on the subject, or talked to your parents, or friends who are parents, about what to expect when you become a parent? You can also learn by babysitting your friends' children, or your nieces and nephews. You'll be a better mom or dad if you go into parenthood with your eyes wide open.

- **Are you prepared financially for raising children? Being a parent is expensive. As**

I said before, the U.S. government estimates that it costs nearly $250,000 to raise a

child from birth to the age of 18. Diapers and formula alone can cost $100 or more every month, and then there are clothes, medicines and doctor visits to deal with fevers, earaches and such. And, those expenses will grow along with your child. I'm not trying to be discouraging. But, again, it is important to know what to expect.

- **How good are you at dealing with the unexpected?**

If you are a person who likes to live an orderly and well-regulated life, or if you believe in "a place for everything and everything in its place," then perhaps you'd better think long and hard before starting a family. Are you annoyed by unexpected interruptions that prevent you from completing all the tasks on your to-do list? You should be aware that, as a parent of a small child, you will have plenty of unexpected interruptions. Babies can't help it if they have colic, need their diapers changed, are going through the pain of teething, or are cranky for some other reason. You can bet that there will be times when you'll put your child down for a long nap, and 15 minutes later, he'll decide, "I've had enough of this." There will be unexpected trips to the doctor to treat bumps and bruises, and spills on your carpet or hardwood floor that need your immediate attention. These are the facts of life for parents everywhere. Most parents deal with these situations gladly – or at least try to – because they love their children so much. Only you know how it would be for you.

Finally, before we leave this topic, I want to mention that you should not let anyone push you into having children. Don't have a baby because your mom wants to be a grandmother, or because your dad is pushing you to give him a fishing buddy. Whether and when to start a family is a decision that should be made by the prospective parents and is no one else's business.

As we've seen, the thirties are a time for taking stock and deciding if we are where we want to be in life, or whether some major changes are called for. It may be a time for making a new start with regard to your marriage, your career, and your family. For most people, the thirties are a time of contentment and growing prosperity. But you can never let your guard down. After all, your forties are on the way.

FOOD FOR THOUGHT

- **Is it time to switch careers?** Do you feel challenged creatively? Is there a clear path to advancement for you? Do you feel appreciated and properly compensated for your work? If your answer to any of these questions is no, then it may be time to move on.
- **Is it time to start a family? Ask yourself:**
- Is your marriage stable? Can it withstand the new pressures that parenting brings?
- Are you and your spouse on the same page when it comes to starting a family?
- How much do you know about raising children?
- Are you prepared financially for raising children?
- Are you good at dealing with the unexpected?
- *Remember:*
- ⊠ e thirties should be a time of figuring out if you're on the right path in life or if some big changes are called for. To do this, you need to step back, take a deep breath and consider whether you are living the life you always wanted.

CHAPTER NINE

THE FORTIES: YOUR LAST CHANCE TO CHANGE YOUR LIFE

Are you old enough to remember the comedian Jack Benny? Benny, who died in 1974, was one of the best-known comedians of the twentieth century, having starred in radio, television and movies.

Throughout his long career, Benny always got a laugh by insisting that he was 39 years old, although he was obviously well past that age. Why 39? Because 39 is young, and 40 is old. Or at least some people see it that way. I have had many people tell me that they couldn't sleep the night before they turned 40 because they were so depressed.

And while I sympathize, I also have some good news. Forty is not old at all. Especially when you consider that the Rolling Stones are still going strong well into their seventies and Tom Brady is setting passing records at 43. Most forty-somethings I know are strong and healthy. Their minds are sharp. They live very active lives. It's true that they're not kids anymore, but neither are they ready for the rest home.

It has been said that life begins at 40, and that has been true for dozens of people like these:[13]

Actor Samuel Jackson landed his first movie acting role at the age of 43.

Vera Wang was 40 and had no fashion experience when she entered the fashion industry and built one of the world's most successful brands.

Henry Ford was 45 when he founded the Ford Motor Company and revolutionized the automobile industry.

Sam Walton opened the first Walmart store in Rogers, Arkansas, at the age of 44.

Julia Child was 50 when she wrote her first cookbook and launched her career as a celebrity chef.

Donald Fisher was 40 when he opened the first Gap store in 1969.

Arianna Hu₵ ngton began the Huffington Post at age 55.

And, according to "Business Insider," research shows that founders of businesses who are

over 40 run more successful companies.

So why, despite the evidence to the contrary, do so many forty-somethings become depressed about the way their lives are going and slip into a mid-life crisis?

Many of the reasons are the same ones that send much younger people into what we called a quarter-life crisis. A feeling that life isn't going in the right direction, and that they're not moving toward fulfilling their dreams.

There may also be the feeling of "It's now or never." In other words, if I don't act now, I never will.

And, actually, this is true. You may be in need of some dramatic changes, and if so, you had better make them now. If you've always wanted to go back to school and get that degree, you'd better do it now. If you want to change your career, there's still time to do that as well. But whatever you do, make sure you've taken the time to think it all out and made solid plans and goals. Don't act impulsively, casting your cares to the wind – because if you do, I can just about guarantee you that you're going to regret it.

Sadly, a lot of forty-somethings who say, "It's now or never," would be better off with "never."

Perhaps you've heard it said, as I have, that the risks you'll regret most in life are the ones you don't take. That sounds good. But it's not a philosophy to build your life on. I've met plenty of people who regret risks they did take. Why? Because those risks ruined their marriages, families, careers and reputations. Cherished things they had built up over many years were destroyed in a matter of days by one impulsive action.

If you are depressed, discontented, and on the verge of doing "something crazy," please share your thoughts with a counselor, clergyman, or a wise friend you can trust. If you are restless and itching for something new and different, look for a positive way to invest that energy.

IT'S NOT YOUR FAULT

One important thing I want you to know about a midlife crisis is that it's not your fault. Over the last decade, research has uncovered the fact that such a crisis is a common psychological problem for people all over the world – and primarily successful people. It happens often enough that it may be tied into our human biology. For example, one study examined people in Peru who had risen out of poverty and were now "enjoying" a successful middle upper-class life. Only they weren't really enjoying it. The study found that people who had always been poor were happier than those who had started out poor but had overcome.

Other researchers found that there is no connection between a country's wealth and the over-all happiness of its residents. At first, as a country's standard of living increases, so does the happiness of its people. But at some point, the correlation reverses. As the economy continues to improve, people become less happy.

This phenomenon is known as the U-Curve, and it is like taking a sudden U-Turn as you're driving at a high speed down the highway of life. Writing about this in the Atlantic Monthly, Jonathan Rauch says, "I was about 50 when I discovered the U-curve and began poking through the growing research on it. What I wish I had known in my 40s (or, even better, in my late 30s is that happiness may be affected by age, and the hard part in middle age, whether you call it a midlife crisis or something else, is for many people a transition to something much better—something, there is reason to hope, like wisdom." [14]

Rauch also writes, "Though I still have my share of gloomy days, I find it far easier than I did in my 40s to appreciate what I have, even without writing down lists of good things, as I had to resort to doing a decade ago. . . . in my 40s, I had plenty of success and none of it seemed adequate, which was why I felt so churlish. For me, after a period when gratitude seemed to have abandoned me, its return feels like a gift."[15]

He also cites research that shows that the usual pattern for those who pass through a mid-life crisis is for joy and happiness to return in their 50s, and continue to increase through the rest of life. So hang on! Your feeling of discontent will not last!

If you have ever seen a psychologist because you were dealing with anxiety, you will know that one of the most important ways you can cope with it is to just let yourself float through it, knowing that it will pass. It can be hard to float through something when you are feeling panicked and as if your heart is about to explode – but it is the very best thing to do. In the same way, you can float through the temptations a mid-life crisis brings your way. Be strong! Don't give in to your fears! This, too, will pass, and you will be much happier if you stay the course.

MORE ON VOLUNTEERING

You may recall that when we talked about the quarter-life crisis, we discussed the importance of giving to others through volunteering. The advice I gave then also pertains to people who are going through a mid-life crisis. In fact, volunteering may be even more important for men and women in their forties, because you have more skills to offer, and you may have more time available to you. In your twenties, you may be doing everything in your power to get your life and career jump-started. You may be working, taking classes, and doing all sorts of other time-consuming things to expand your skills and increase your worth to your employer, or prospective employer.

In your forties, you may be in a solid position in your company that allows you more time for volunteering. You may not have any more "leisure time" than you did in your twenties, especially if you have children. But because you are more secure in your job, you may feel freer to volunteer. Volunteering is important because as you help others, you will feel better about yourself, which means you will feel less disappointed and frustrated about the way your life has turned out. Focusing on the needs of others will help you take your eyes off yourself, and that is a key to diminishing psychological (and physical) pain.

How do you decide where to volunteer?

First, figure out how many hours you can give without overcommitting or overburdening yourself.

en, ask yourself where your passions lie. Would you like to help animals, work with children, assist the elderly, provide meals for hungry people, combat homelessness, protect the environment, help teach adults to read and write, work in a school, serve in your church, provide after-school tutoring for at-risk kids, etc. As you see, the possibilities are virtually endless. You can almost certainly connect your passions to a volunteer opportunity.

Finally, ask if there is a way to use your skills as a volunteer. If you are an accountant, you may help to keep the books, if you are a writer, you may help prepare promotional materials, and so on. But it is just as likely that you will want to do something completely different from what you do on the job.

This is one of the beauties of organizations like Habitat for Humanity, which bring people together from all professions and walks of life to build homes for low-income families. Many people who spend their normal work-day in an office in the corporate world are able to get outside and work with their hands for a change, and they find great pleasure in it.

WHY CAN'T I SLEEP?

One of the biggest complaints I hear from people in their forties is, "I just don't get enough sleep." If getting enough sleep is a problem for you, you can take some comfort in the fact that you are not alone. According to the U.S. Centers for Disease Control and Prevention, nearly one-third of

American adults are sleep-deprived.[16] In other words, 40 million men and women are not getting the sleep they need to operate at maximum efficiency. It's pretty scary to realize that one out of every three drivers you pass on the road each day is sleepy!

There are several reasons why getting a good night's sleep is harder for people in their forties. For one thing, you may have trouble sleeping through the night. You wake up to make a quick trip to the bathroom and then can't get back to sleep, or wake up an hour or more before your alarm clock is set to go off. You may not be getting enough exercise, especially if you sit at a desk all day at work. At the same time, your body is losing hormones that promote good sleep. Lack of these hormones can cause you to crave starchy and fatty foods which will result in weight gain. Almost before you know it, you can be in the grip of full-blown insomnia.

What can you do to prevent this from happening? First, be sure you are getting enough exercise. Second, eat a healthy diet, and don't eat or drink anything within three hours of your bedtime. You can also make sure that your bedroom is quiet and dark. Some people keep the TV on all night, and doze off and on, but that's not good enough. I find it very helpful to have a specific bedtime, when the TV is turned off and the lights go out. You may also want to practice stress management through yoga, taking a quiet walk in the early evening, or working with a therapist.

If you do have insomnia and can't seem to shake it, I suggest that you see a competent psychologist or sleep doctor. There are several medications that can help you get a good night's sleep, so don't suffer unnecessarily. And if your spouse says you snore, or if you are always tired, you might want to get checked for sleep apnea. This is an insidious condition that can steal your energy and your life, but it is treatable.

Insomnia can be very difficult, especially if you've always been the sort of person who falls asleep almost as soon as your head hits the pillow. A sudden inability to get the sleep you need can leave you virtually unable to function, and you can reach the point where you think you'll never sleep again. One man told me that he felt a sense of dread every afternoon as soon as the sun began to go down. He was literally afraid that he would spend another night tossing and turning in bed, trying to get a few hours of sleep. I have heard of people who killed themselves because they were suffering from insomnia. And remember that Michael Jackson's death was indirectly related to insomnia – and it came just two months short of his forty-first birthday. Such tragedies are heartbreaking and unnecessary. Help is available!

FOOD FOR THOUGHT

- **Are you restless** and itching for something new and different? Look for a positive way to invest that energy.

Remember:

- **Research has uncovered the fact** that the mid-life crisis is a common psychological problem for people all over the world – and primarily successful people. It happens often enough that it may be tied into our human biology.
- **Learn to float** through the temptations a mid-life crisis brings your way. Be strong! Don't give in to your fears! This, too, will pass, and you will be happier if you stay the course.
- **Insomnia is a common and sometimes severe problem** for people in their forties and fifties. If it affects you, don't suffer in silence. Seek help from a competent psychiatrist, psychologist or sleep doctor.

PART FIVE
HEADED DOWN THE
HOME STRETCH

13 Richard Feloni and Alana Akhtar, "24 people who became highly successful after age 40," businessinsider.com, January 16, 2020 14 Johnathan Rauch, "The Real Roots of Midlife Crisis," Atlantic Monthly, November, 2014

Rauch, Atlantic Monthly, November 2014

"Nearly a third of Americans are sleep deprived," www.medicaldaily.com, April 27, 2012

CHAPTER TEN

GOING STRONG IN YOUR FIFTIES AND SIXTIES

In our youth-oriented culture, turning fifty can be tough. And sixty is even worse! These are the years when you will receive your membership card from AARP (American Association of Retired People, whether you want it or not. You can also count on younger clerks and salespeople to say condescending things to you in an attempt to be nice. And there are times when your body will remind you that you're no longer twenty.

A friend of mine told me about going into a fast-food restaurant for a bit of lunch, and noticing that the cashier had undercharged him $3.00.

He went back to the young man at the cashier, showed him the receipt and said, "I think I owe you a few dollars."

"No sir," the cashier smiled. "That's your senior discount." Ouch!

You have to forgive the kids. To them, anyone past their forties looks like Methuselah.

But the truth is that 50 is a much younger age than it has ever been at any other time in history. It may be a cliché that fifty is the new thirty, but as with most clichés, there's quite a bit of truth in that. There are some great things about being in your fifties, and these include:

•By the time you reach your fifties you have the wisdom and experience to know what's important in life and let the rest go.

•Your children have grown up and – hopefully – become the people you always wanted them to be.

•You no longer have to keep up with the latest fashions – especially those that are uncomfortable, expensive and – let's admit it – silly looking.

•You can get senior discounts. Many restaurants, hotels and other businesses offer discounts starting at age 55. Some people say they don't want to take them because it hurts their pride. They say they don't need any extra help. And yet, these discounts can save you quite a bit of money, so why not take them?

•You have wisdom gained through experience. People listen to you because they believe you know what you're talking about. (If they don't, that's their problem, not yours. And they'll find out sooner or later that you were right.)

•You have more freedom to do the things you really want to do. You may not be completely free of responsibilities and obligations, but as your children grow up, you should have more time for yourself. You can spend more time reading, take day-trips to interesting places in your community, go fishing, take up gardening, travel, or just about anything your heart desires – as long as you have the money to do it.

These are just a few of the joys that can come from being in your sixties. But then again, it's not all flowers and rainbows by any stretch of the imagination. Your fifties may bring on aches and pains and a loss of stamina. Now, more than ever before, you need to take care of your mind and body. If you have a persistent physical issue, get it checked out by a doctor. Don't just sit and wait and hope it will go away. And you can't just sit on the

couch and watch Netflix. You must exercise your body and your mind. Read, play brain games, do crossword puzzles or Sudoku. The old saying, "Use it or lose it" applies to your body and your brain.

It's also extremely important to have a positive perception of yourself and your age. Studies have found that people who maintain a positive perception of aging live longer than others – by an average of more than seven years. One of the reasons for this seems to be that they value themselves more and thus take better care of themselves. This is just

another piece of evidence to show that emotional and physical health go hand in hand. So, don't put yourself down – and don't let anyone else do it either. As Ashton Applewhite writes, "Condescension alone actually shortens lives. What professionals call 'elderspeak,' – the belittling 'sweeties' and 'dearies' – that people use to address older people — does more than rankle. It reinforces stereotypes of incapacity and incompetence, which leads to poorer health, including shorter life spans."[17]

She goes on to say, "Overaccommodation also harms – behavior like using simpler words and sentences, or speaking louder and more slowly than we would to a younger person, instead of first ascertaining that the person is, in fact confused or hard of hearing. Targets of this demeaning behavior appear to 'instantly age,' speaking, moving and thinking less capably."[18]

Here are some of the other specific issues you may face in your fifties:

You may feel fatigued. If this is the case with you, please don't write it off and say, "Of course, I'm tired, I've worked hard all my life." For your own sake, you need to deal with any issues that are pulling you down. There may be psychological issues, such as depression or anxiety, that are causing you to feel exhausted. If your tired feeling is mingled with feelings of sadness, sorrow, and regret, you should seek out the help of a respected therapist. There may also be physical issues involved, such as sleep apnea, or an absence of important nutrients your body needs to function properly. Perhaps you're not getting enough rest or sufficient exercise. If you are tired all the time, don't write it off as being attributed to old age – because you are nowhere near old age in your fifties.

You may need to change your diet. There are a number of physical issues that can crop up when you're in your fifties or older, and some of these – maybe even most — are linked in some way to poor nutrition. For example, hypertension may be related to diet that is high in salt, so use salt in moderation. Caffeine can contribute to a lack of sleep, so you might want to cut back on consumption of coffee, tea and caffeinated sodas. We all know the serious problems that can come from use of tobacco, alcohol and too much red meat. I'm not trying to give you a primer on proper nutrition or behavior. That's far beyond my scope. But you will stay young longer and live better if you treat your body right — and because physical and mental health are related, you will also be happier. Often, a few changes can make a big difference. For instance, if you eat well and cut back on caffeine and salt, you'll probably sleep better. If you sleep better, you'll feel better – and that will give you a more positive outlook on life.

Remember that an ounce of prevention is worth a pound of cure. Nobody wants to fill their schedule with doctor's visits. But there are several preventive tests and procedures that should be started when you're in your fifties. They may seem like a nuisance now but could save you lots of trouble later on.

These include mammograms for women and prostate exams for men. You should also get a colonoscopy, a sleep test if you

think you might be dealing with sleep apnea, and a bone-density screening. You might also want to get your heart checked and, if you have moles or freckles, a visit to a dermatologist is not a bad idea. You may not need all of these tests, so ask your GP what he thinks, and follow his or her advice.

Don't let go of your purpose. Sometimes, people in their fifties start counting the days until retirement, and that's okay as long as you want to retire so you can spend more time doing something that really excites you. It's not okay if you want to retire so you spend more time on the sofa watching the latest offerings from Netflix or Prime Video. Having a purpose in life is important to your health and longevity, so please, for your own sake, don't let go of your dreams. You are NOT too old to make a difference.

Joan Raymond, writing in Today.com, has this to say about purpose:[19]

"Purpose" provides structure to our lives, said psychiatrist Niranjan Karnik, M.D. of Rush University Medical Center. And when retirement or other age-related challenges loom, some individuals may lose their sense of "purpose" and positivity, leading to poor health and poorer sense of well-being, he adds.

Having "purpose" in midlife and beyond doesn't mean you have to strive to change the world — although if you think you can, why not try? Rather, ". . . it's simply finding meaning in the day to day," whether that's gardening, learning a new language, volunteering at a local pet shelter or even starting a new career if you want, said Karnik.

You may not be quite as sharp as you used to be. But that doesn't necessarily mean there's anything wrong with you, or that you're heading down the road to Alzheimer's or dementia. When you stop by the ATM, does it sometimes take you a couple of seconds to remember your password? Or have you ever been asked for your phone number and blanked out? More than likely it's because you've got too much information in your brain, so it can take you a little bit longer to access the information you need. But you can cut down on the frequency of these events and prevent memory loss by getting plenty of exercise. MRIs show that adults who exercise regularly have a bigger hippocampus (the brain region responsible for memory and learning), which helps keep the mind sharp. If you are feeling forgetful, just remember that when you reach your fifties the transmission of nerve impulses slows down slightly – but it's nothing to worry about unless it happens every day and seems to be getting worse. If that's the case, it's time to see your doctor.

Ashton Applewhite, who I've quoted before, says in her book, *ff is Chair Rocks: A manifesto Against Ageism,* that anxiety over memory loss is a bigger problem than memory loss itself. She points out that 90 percent of adults over the age of 65 "can think just fine."[20] Furthermore, she says that as the American population ages, the percentage of those with dementia is decreasing. It is a fact that more Americans are staying healthy in mind and body, far into what we used to call "old age."

Forgive and forget. Are you holding a grudge against someone? By the time you turn 50, you are likely to have a fairly long list of people who have wronged you in some way. But is there someone you just can't forgive? Perhaps even someone who hurt you 20 or 25 years ago? If so, you've held onto that grudge way too long. It's time to let it go. It will make you feel better and happier as you move into the future. My personal observation is that resentment and unforgiveness can add years to your age. You may be thinking, "But I just can't make up my mind to forgive." My answer is, "Yes, you can." Forgiving someone is an act of your will. Decide you're going to do it and then do it.

Is it necessary to tell someone you forgive them? No! Especially if the other person involved doesn't even know you're angry with them. There is no reason to open old wounds. Nor should you resume a relationship with someone who has a toxic personality. In other words, don't put yourself in a position to let someone who has already hurt you do it again. But if you have let some trivial misunderstanding come between you and a well-meaning person you once cared about, it's time to make an attempt at restoring that relationship.

What if the person who wounded you is deceased. In that case, I suggest writing them a letter to express your forgiveness, and then burn it. The purpose of this is to set yourself free from the pain resentment and unforgiveness can cause.

Hang onto the people that matter the most to you, and let the others go. It sounds counterintuitive, but some researchers have found that the happiest "older people" are not necessarily those with the most friends. Instead, they have cut back on the number of their relationships so they can concentrate their attention on the people who mean the most to them. It seems that good friendships are important, but "good" is the operative word. It may sound cruel to talk about jettisoning friendships, and that's not exactly what I'm talking about. I am talking about spending more time with people you care about, and less time with people who drain your energy and leave you feeling worn out.

This makes me think of a friend of mine who has a difficult time with Facebook. When he first went on Facebook, he began getting friend requests from people he had known over the years – most of them co-workers and classmates from years ago. He barely remembered some of these people. They weren't really what you'd call "friends," but he didn't want to hurt their feelings so he accepted their requests. Now, he has nearly 300 "friends," only a handful of which he's really close to. He doesn't have anything much in common with the rest of the folks.

Whenever he logs onto Facebook, which isn't often, he has to wade through a bunch of posts from people he doesn't really know about things that aren't really important to him. It's a drain and, for that reason, he doesn't check into Facebook very often, and he sometimes misses important news from people he really does care about. The moral of the story is that if you have too many friends, you can't really be a friend to any of them.

Of course, it's fine to have plenty of acquaintances. But it's far better to have two or three good friends rather than dozens of "friends" you barely know.

FOOD FOR THOUGHT

- **Author Ashton Applewhite** says anxiety over memory loss is a bigger problem than memory loss itself. Do you agree? Why or why not.
- **Do you think it's possible** to have too many friends? Why or why not?

Remember:

- **Gray hair is a badge of honor.** Wear it proudly.
- **When you are in your fifties and sixties, you must exercise your body and your mind.** Read, play brain games, do crossword puzzles or Sudoku. The old saying, "Use it or lose it" applies to your body and your brain.
- **It's extremely important to have a positive perception of yourself and your age.** Studies have found that people who maintain a positive perception of aging live longer than others – by an average of more than seven years.

---

[17] Applewhite, Ashton, "This Chair Rocks: A Manifesto Against Ageism, "(Celadon Books: New York) 2019, Page 19 [18] Applewhite, Page 19

[19] Joan Raymond, "The 6 biggest health mistakes women make in their 50s," www.today.com/health, October 23, 2015 [20] Applewhite, Page 5.

CHAPTER ELEVEN

THE SEVENTIES AND BEYOND: A TIME TO LOVE

The Beatles said it nearly fifty years ago:

"In the end, the love you take, is equal to the love you make."

These words are very true, and it's sad that most people don't realize it until they are heading toward the final turn in the race of life. So many people I've counseled over the years started out in life thinking they were put here to help themselves – to money, pleasure, and anything else they wanted. But as they age, they are surprised to discover that they were put here to help others instead of themselves. I don't want to preach, but I also want to urge you not to wait too long to make that discovery for yourself.

Your latter years should be a time when you take stock of your life and let your friends and family members know how important they are to you. In case you never realized it before, let me tell you that death is inevitable. It may not come to you for another 30 years or more. After all, there is a great deal of research into extending the human life span. Over the last few decades, the average life expectancy here in the United States has steadily climbed up to 79.8 years. (Surprisingly, 41 countries are ahead of us.) But now, there is talk of a quantum leap forward, to 120 or beyond. So, a seventy-year-old may have quite a while left.

But whenever your time comes, if you are a person who has given of yourself to others, you can go out with great joy!

George Burns used to say that the first thing he did every morning was read the obituaries in the newspaper. If his obituary wasn't in there, he ate breakfast. It's funny, but almost true. I used to wonder why anyone would read the obituary page. How morbid! But as I get older, I find myself reading the obituaries more and more. And it still shocks me to find that so many men and women who are younger than I have died. It makes me think of my own mortality, and about what is most important to me – and that's my relationships with people I really care about. Coming face to face with my own mortality makes me realize how important it is for me to let my favorite people know how much I care about them – and it makes me want to rediscover and rebuild lost relationships, if possible.

Here are some things you can do to help make sure your golden years really are golden — that you finish strong like an Olympic champion sprinting across the finish line.

GET YOUR AFFAIRS IN ORDER

I understand that life never comes in neat little packages. There are always some loose ends, a bit of unfinished business.

Still, it's important to tidy things up as much as possible. So do your best to deal with loose ends like hurt feelings, misunderstandings, arguments or grudges that have never been dealt with. If there is something you need to say, say it now before it's too late. If there's something you should do, do it now.

But, of course, getting your affairs in order also has a practical side. Have you made plans for your funeral and burial so it doesn't fall on those who will be bereaved by your passing?

Have you cleaned out your garage or your closets to get rid of things you don't really need so your kids won't have to deal with them? You don't want them to have to spend hours cleaning out items that should have been discarded years ago – so do it now.

I know this sounds kind of morbid, like I am telling you to prepare for death, but that's not because death is imminent. I really think we should always be prepared. After all, death is inevitable.

TAKE CARE OF THOSE YOU LOVE

You might consider this to be a continuation of "Get Your Affairs in Order." Do you have a will or a living trust? If so, is it current? If the answer to either one of these questions is no, take care of it now. Don't put it off until tomorrow, because tomorrow may be too late.

Drawing up a will is important for many reasons. It's not only a means through which you can "bless" each of your heirs in the way you see fit, but can also be used to provide extra help for those who are disabled or have other special needs. A will can help your children avoid a lengthy probate process, and allows you to leave bequests to churches, schools, or charities that mean a great deal to you.

These are just some of the many important reasons for having a will, and I'm sure I'm not telling you anything you don't already know. My purpose here is to push you to remind you of those reasons, so that if you don't have a will or a living trust, you'll move forward to get it done now.

I would also suggest that you sit down with your children beforehand – so long as they are trustworthy – and give them a basic understanding of what your estate looks like. Surely, you don't want any distressing surprises at the reading of your will, or family squabbles later down the road.

What else can you do to take care of the people you love? Maybe you'll want to leave each of your heirs a letter, telling how much you love them. Or pick out one special item you want to leave each of them — something that speaks of your special relationship with each one.

I suggest you spend some time thinking of ways you can ensure that the people you care about feel your special love for them long after you are no longer here to tell them yourself.

REMEMBER, YOU ARE LOVED

Have you ever spent some time thinking about all the people who have loved you? If not, why not take the time to do it now? Sit down and make a list. It may sound a bit silly, or self-indulgent, but it's not. It is actually a good way to think about the difference you've made, and are making, in this world.

So, who has loved you? Some of the people you put on your list would be:

Your spouse.

Your parents. (This can be your biological or adoptive parents. If you are adopted, then I hope you can find joy in the fact that your parents chose you. You were the one they wanted.)

Your grandparents.

Your brothers and sisters.

Aunts and uncles.

Nieces and nephews.

Other people who might go on your list include your best friend or friends from childhood.

Did you have a teacher who really took an interest in you and helped you succeed in school? Put him or her on your list. Or perhaps there was a Sunday school teacher, a scout leader, or some other person who cared about you and made a positive impact on your life.

How about your first girlfriend or boyfriend?

Your best friend from high school or college?

Spend some time thinking about this. There may be some people you've forgotten about over the years who once made a huge difference in your life. As they come to mind, add them to your list. Then spend some time reflecting on your relationship with these people. But don't waste any of that time brooding about regrets. I don't want you to start thinking about why you and your first love broke up, or about the time your grandfather got mad at you because you broke his window with a baseball. Concentrate on positive memories and see the joy you have brought into other people's lives.

I'm sure you've seen the classic Christmas movie, *It's a Wonderful Life.* (I doubt very much if there's anyone old enough to be reading this book who hasn't seen this movie. It's on TV dozens of times every Christmas season.)

In the film, a character named George Bailey decides to take his life because he thinks the world would be better off without him. But as he contemplates jumping from a bridge, he encounters an angel, who shows him what the world would really be like without him – and it's not a very happy place. Bailey is encouraged to see the positive difference he's made, decides not to jump off the bridge, and everything works out fine.

Now, I'm not saying that you feel like a failure – why should you? – or even that you're depressed. But neither are you likely to meet a guardian angel who's going to show you what a positive difference you've made – so you might as well make up your own list. Just knowing that you've been loved by so many people should help you realize that you've had a pretty good life, and enable you to walk into the future with a smile on your face and your head held high.

Encouragement is so important to all of us. In the first chapters of this book, we discussed about the importance of encouraging our children in order to build the confidence they need to succeed in life. However, unlike Trix — the breakfast cereal that has always advertised itself as being only for kids – encouragement is important for people of all ages. Everyone needs to receive encouragement, and everyone needs to give it.

That's why, after you've made a list of the people who have loved you, I want you to reverse the process and make another list of the people you have loved. The list may be the same, but it may be completely different. We're not talking here about every cute member of the opposite sex you've ever had a crush on, or everyone you've ever dated. Rather, I am talking about people who touched your life in a deep and lasting way. Once you have your list, if the people on it are still alive and available to you, why not write them a short email telling them how much you have always appreciated them?

A man once told me about a friend's mother who was very good to him when he was a boy. He always called her "Aunt Ruth." She treated him kindly and he always felt welcome in her home. He ate many meals in his friend's home, enjoyed sleepovers there, and was taken on outings to places like the zoo, amusement parks, etc. and more.

He came from a good home where he was loved and cared for. It wasn't as if Aunt Ruth came to his rescue because he

was in need. She was a happy part of his childhood because he genuinely felt that she cared about him.

I suggested he write to her and tell her how much he appreciated all she did for him. He followed my advice, and he told me later how good it made him feel. At this time, Ruth was in her late 80s. A few months after receiving the letter, she passed away. My friend says that he is so glad he wrote that letter, that it was one of the few times in his life that he said what he needed to say before it was too late. I urge you to follow his example. My philosophy is, "If someone is important to you, or has made a positive impact on your life, let him or her know how you feel." I think that's a good rule to follow."

Understand that I am not talking about writing to old flames, and especially not if they are now married to someone else. In that situation, I'm afraid your intentions may be misinterpreted. The last thing you want to do is stir up jealous feelings on the part of someone's husband or wife.

Use your common sense and things will be just fine, and you'll feel good knowing that you've put smiles on some old friends' faces by letting them know how much they mean to you.

REACH OUT TO YOUNG PEOPLE

Several studies have found that one of the best ways to stay young in your "golden years" is to associate with younger people. That's why I think it's sad that, as soon as they reach the age of 55, so many Americans pack up and move into communities for Senior Citizens. These are places where the musical sound of children's laughter is never heard, where there are no little boys and girls playing in front yards. Silence can be a good thing, but too much silence can feel like the sound of death.

I understand the lure of these "55 and Over" communities. Many of them are filled with amenities like swimming pools, spas, theaters, tennis courts and golf courses, and housing prices may be lower. However, without any cross-generational relationships, you may find yourself sinking into old age faster than you want to. George Vaillant, a Harvard professor, says, "Those in middle age and beyond who invest in caring for and developing the next generation are three times as likely to be happy as those who fail to do so." According Vaillant, "We're wired to connect with those younger than we are and to help create a better future. It's good for us psychologically, and in every other way."[21]

Before, we move on, here are seven ideas from Harvard University to help you keep your memory strong "at any age."[22]

1. Keep learning

Challenging your brain with mental exercise is believed to strengthen individual brain cells and stimulate communication among them. It's important to make lifelong learning a priority.

2. Use all your senses

The more senses you use in learning something, the more of your brain will be involved in retaining the memory. So, challenge all your senses as you venture into the unfamiliar.

3. Believe in yourself

Older learners do worse on memory tasks when they're exposed to negative stereotypes about aging and memory, and better when the messages are positive about memory preservation into old age. This is yet another example of the importance of encouragement.

4. Economize your brain use

Take advantage of calendars and planners, maps, shopping lists, and similar materials to keep routine information accessible to you. Albert Einstein once admitted that he didn't know how many feet there are in a mile. He said he didn't want to clutter up his brain with information that was so easy to look up. Another good idea is to have a designated place at home for glasses, keys, and other items you use often.

5. Repeat what you want to know

When you want to remember something you've just heard, read, or thought about, repeat it out loud or write it down. That way, you reinforce the memory or connection.

6. Space it out

Repetition is most potent as a learning tool when it's properly timed. It's best not to repeat something many times in a short period, as if you were cramming for an exam. Instead, re-study the essentials after increasingly longer periods of time — once an hour, then every few hours, then every day.

7. Make a mnemonic

This is a creative way to remember lists. For example, you can remember the order of the planets in our solar system with the mnemonic "My very excited mother just served us nachos." (Mercury, Venus, Earth, Mars, Jupiter, Saturn, Uranus, Neptune.)

****

This concludes our time together. It has been brief, but I trust that this small volume has been helpful to you.

When we started out on this journey, I said that the process of building a successful life begins in early childhood – and even before birth, but it goes on for the rest of our lives. It's never too late to make up for past mistakes and errors of judgment; overcome damage caused by bullies, false friends, and careless parents, and get on the right track in life.

I wish you love and blessings on the road ahead.

May the words of the old Irish blessing come true for you:

May the road riseup to meet you.

May the wind be always at your back. May the sun shine warm upon your face; the rains fall soft upon your fields and until we meet again, may God hold you in the palm of His hand.

And finally, I want to leave you with a simple truth that was shared with me by one of the best and most effective mentors I ever had:

"In the end, what matters most is how many people you have loved, and how many have loved you back."

FOOD FOR THOUGHT

•Encouragement is extremely important. What can you do or say to encourage the people you see every day?

•Harvard professor George Vaillant says, "Those in middle age and beyond who invest in caring for and developing the next generation are three times as likely to be happy as those who fail to do so." Why do you think this is true? What can you do to invest in and care for the next generation?

•Name three people who have had a major positive impact on your life.
Remember:

•Your latter years should be a time when you take stock of your life and let your friends and family members know how important they are to you.

•Make a list of some of the ways you can do this.

[21] Freedman, Marc, "How to Live Forever: The Enduring Power of Connecting the Generations," (New York: Public Affairs) 2018, Page 32 [22] Adapted from, "7 ways to keep your memory sharp at any age," www.health.harvard.edu

www.ingramcontent.com/pod-product-compliance
Lightning Source LLC
Chambersburg PA
CBHW051002140626
46546CB00017B/2452